The Lorimer Pocketguide to

# *Toronto*
# Birds

*120 Species in Full Colour*

Written & illustrated by
Jeffrey C. Domm

James Lorimer & Company Ltd., Publishers
Toronto, Ontario
2002

*Dedicated to Mary Lou and Bob, my parents, for their support and encouragement.*

James Lorimer & Company Ltd. acknowledges the support of the Ontario Arts Council. We acknowledge the financial support of the Government of Canada through the Book Publishing Industry Development Program (BPIDP) for our publishing activities.

**National Library of Canada Cataloguing in Publication**

Domm, Jeffrey C., 1958-
        The Lorimer pocketguide to Toronto birds : 120 species in full colour /
written & illustrated by Jeffrey C. Domm.

Includes index.
ISBN 1-55028-772-9


        1. Birds—Ontario—Toronto—Identification. 2. Bird watching—Ontario—Toronto—Guidebooks. I. Title.

QL685.5.O6D656 2002          598'.09713'541          C2002-903781-6

Cartography: Peggy McCalla

James Lorimer & Company, Publishers
35 Britain Street
Toronto, Ontario M5A 1R7
www.lorimer.ca

Printed and bound in Canada

# Introduction

This book is designed to help you identify birds quickly and easily. Each species is given one full page, which includes a colour illustration as well as keys to correct identification of birds seen in the Toronto area. The illustrations are drawn from several sources, including photographs, observations and scientific data. They emphasize the distinguishing features — shape, colour and markings — and each one represents a typical specimen. One should expect to see variation in the colour of a bird's plumage — variation that results from changing seasons and light conditions.

To identify a bird, use the 2-step Bird Finder on pages 4-5, which organizes the species by size and by colour. To become familiar with the graphic symbols used in this book see the "How to use this guide" section on pages 6-7.

Of the more than 400 species recorded in southern Ontario, we have selected 120 familiar birds for this book. They are organized in the taxonomic sequence presented by the American Ornithologists' Union. The wetland and water birds precede the woodland and field birds. Make your own record of bird sightings on the checklist (pages 138-145).

Before setting out on a bird watching excursion, check the weather forecasts. If a storm moves in very quickly, strong winds, rain and cool temperatures can affect the number of birds that you see and can dampen spirits on your expedition. Always take along waterproof clothing as well as your binoculars. For this book, a local Toronto birding expert has provided information on Hot Spot Birding Locations that are favoured by local enthusiasts.

Birds of all sizes play an important role in the balance of nature, but their survival is increasingly threatened by unnatural incursions. Preserving habitat diversity is becoming vital as human encroachment extends farther into wildlands. Wetlands have declined because of drainage, farming and urbanization, while forests have been harvested and replaced with housing, roads and industrial development. In addition, habitat has been affected by exotic diseases, alien insects and invasive plants. One of the greatest threats to songbirds is the domestic cat.

This book is intended to expand awareness about birds and their place in nature. You can find out more about local birds and their habitat by contacting one of the many organizations dedicated to their preservation and protection. The Toronto Ornithological Club operates a very helpful website: www.torontobirding.ca.

# 2-Step Bird Finder: Size and Colour

Step 1. Determine the approximate size of bird in relation to page size.
Step 2. Compare overall colour and specific markings and turn to page number.

125 134
43 96
66 65
58 130
40 98
60 73
48 49
74 51
129 99
77 68

53 46
35 41
33 27
37 44
50 25
30 78
69 131
59 56
57 64
34 32

23 24
54 38
21 22
61 29
31 45
20 55
42 26
47 18
36 39
28 19

5

# How to use this guide

Birds don't stay in one place for very long, so it is important to learn a few simple rules to help you identify them quickly. Most often what you see is a bird that is feeding; perhaps it is hopping along the ground or flitting from branch to branch. Maybe it is perched in a tree, preparing to fly away at any second. The visual keys given in this guide focus on the most identifiable features of each bird — colour, outline and size. In addition, there are other behavioural traits that help identify birds at a distance. For inland birds, nesting location is an important indicator of habitat. For shore and water birds, the way the bird feeds and the style of flying are helpful hints.

When you are looking at a bird, first estimate the size, then take note of the shape of the wings, tail, head, beak and feet. Note any particular marks — patches, streaks, stripes and speckles. Watch its movements to see how it flies, hops and feeds.

## Legend for visual keys

**1 Size identification** — the rectangle represents the page of this book, and the silhouette of the bird represents its size against this page.

**2 Beak** — the shape of the beak and head can be very helpful in identifying a bird.

**3 Flight characteristics —**

Quick wingbeats

Slow steady wingbeats

Soaring

Wingbeats followed by gliding

**4** Feeding technique —

Stabs and prodding motion

Grazing and dabbling

Diving and clutching with feet

Diving head first

Dives from water's surface

Tip up feeding

Skims water surface

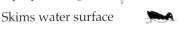

Feeding

**5** **Backyard feeder** — there are two types of bird feeders to which small birds might be attracted.

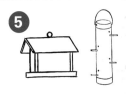

Backyard Feeder

**6** **Birdhouse nester** — some species are happy to make their nest in a manmade house that you hang in your garden.

**7** **Nesting location** (for inland birds only) —

▼ Hollow in ground

▼ Waterside plants

▽ Bushes and thickets

▼ Cavities of trees

▼ Deciduous trees

▽ Conifers and tall trees

▼ Tall, dead, decaying trees

▼ Banks along rivers and ponds

▽ Cliffs and/or rocky ledges

Birdhouse Nester

Nesting Location

**8** **Egg** — actual size and shape unless otherwise indicated.

**9** **Observation calendar** — the bar provides the initial for each of the 12 months of the year. The deeper colour indicates the best months for seeing the species, according to known migration patterns.

Observation Calendar
J F M A M J J A S O N D

Egg: 75%

# Toronto Birding Hot Spots selected by Hugh Currie

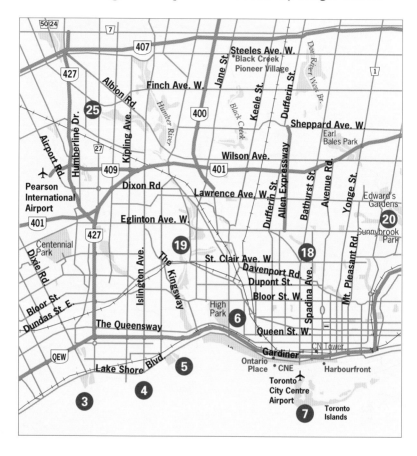

## 1 Paletta/McNichol/Shoreacres Park

Paletta has been the name of this park since 2001. It is a large estate that was taken over by the city for taxes. While the manicured lawns have little in the way of birds, the wooded areas to the east are good, and one can enjoy a fine view of Lake Ontario. On the walk along the wood-chip trail to the lake, you can often spot woodpeckers and wrens, as well as migrants during spring and fall. Buffleheads can be seen on the lake from November to March. The park is about halfway between Walker's Line and Appleby Line in Burlington, on the south side of Lakeshore Road. There is a circular trail, about one kilometre in length, with bridges that cross Shoreacres Creek at both the north and south ends.

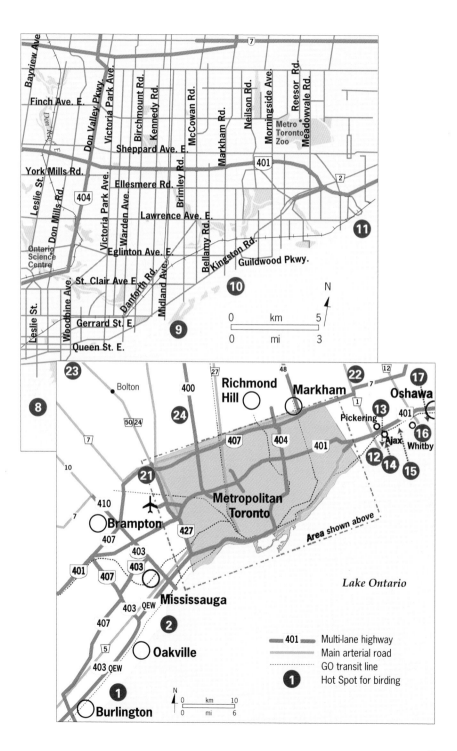

Finch Ave. E.

Bayview Ave.
Don Valley Pkwy.
Victoria Park Ave.
Birchmount Rd.
Kennedy Rd.
McCowan Rd.
Markham Rd.
Neilson Rd.
Morningside Ave.
Reesor Rd.
Meadowvale Rd.

7

Metro Toronto Zoo

Sheppard Ave. E.

York Mills Rd.

401

2

Ellesmere Rd.

404

Leslie St.
Don Mills Rd.
Victoria Park Ave.
Warden Ave.
Brimley Rd.

Lawrence Ave. E.

Ontario Science Centre

Eglinton Ave. E.

Bellamy Rd.
Kingston Rd.

Guildwood Pkwy.

11

St. Clair Ave E.

Danforth Rd.
Midland Ave.

10

N

Woodbine Ave.
Leslie St.

Gerrard St. E.

9

0    km    5
0    mi    3

Queen St. E.

23

Bolton

27

400

Richmond Hill

48

Markham

22

7

12

17

Oshawa

8

50 24

24

7

Pickering

1

13

401

10

407

404

401

16

Whitby

21

Ajax

12

14

15

410

Brampton

407

427

Metropolitan Toronto

Area shown above

403

403

QEW

Mississauga

401

407

407

2

5

Oakville

Lake Ontario

403 QEW

1

401    Multi-lane highway
        Main arterial road
        GO transit line
    1   Hot Spot for birding

N

0    km    10
0    mi    6

Burlington

9

## ② Rattray's Marsh

At this birding destination, you will find fairly extensive woods and a marsh with a viewing platform, allowing you to see the ducks and shorebirds. Canada Geese are often present on the lake and the woods are excellent for birds year-round. Exit the Queen Elizabeth Way at Mississauga Road, and go south to Lakeshore Road. Go right (west) on Lakeshore for three kilometres to Bexhill Road, then left (south) on Bexhill for 0.8 kilometres. Near the parking lot, you will see a map of the area.

## ③ Marie Curtis Park

The lawns here are vast, and the park is bisected by Etobicoke Creek. Marie Curtis offers an opportunity to see waterfowl from close up at the feeding area at the river. Farther west, there is an extensive woodland, which is good for migrants. Sometimes owls can be found here as well. Much of these woods are private property, but the huge gaps in the fence and the many trails suggest that there is no problem birding here. From Dixie Road at Lakeshore Road, go 0.4 kilometres east, then turn right (south) to the park.

## ④ Colonel Samuel Smith Park

This landfill has been improved to add ponds and marshes, and there is a viewing platform. If you walk all the way to the end, you may find Horned Larks and other winter birds during that season. The ponds and marshes are good for ducks and rails, while the huge old spruce trees to the north are often excellent for migratory birds. Check also the old orchard to the west of the rows of spruce trees. From the Queen Elizabeth Way, go south on Kipling Avenue past Lakeshore Road to the parking lot close to the lake.

## ⑤ Humber Bay East and West Parks

Both of these large parks have close-cut lawns, but the east portion of Humber Bay East has been allowed to grow rank. As the bushes and trees continue to mature, the birding will improve. On both of these artificially created peninsulas, waterfowl can be seen at close range, and there has been some landscaping on Humber Bay East, which attracts ducks to the shoreline. Humber Bay West offers a good view of the bay to the north. From the parking lot near the base of Humber Bay West, walk west along the boardwalk to the gazebo and beyond. In winter, many gulls can be seen from here, roosting on the yacht club docks. These parks can be reached by the Queen streetcar, or by exiting the Gardiner Expressway at Park Lawn Road and going south to the lake.

## 6 High Park

This huge park is undergoing restoration to its original vegetation. Check the marsh at the north end of Grenadier Pond for rails, then the pond itself. Continue up the hill, past the Grenadier Restaurant, to Colborne Lodge. Walk east from here to the duck ponds, then north along Spring Road. In the fall, join the hawk-watchers on the hill, just north of the restaurant. The park is easily reached by the TTC subway. Go to High Park station, then walk south across Bloor Street. If driving, park near the north entrance, walk west, then south along the trails.

## 7 Toronto Islands

An entire day is needed to fully explore the islands. The best birding area is the Island Nature Sanctuary (not signposted) just north of the Island Nature School. One should also check the beaches, on the west and south sides, for shorebirds and ducks. The woods south of the Ward's Island village can be good for migrants. Ferries leave from the foot of Bay Street going to Hanlan's Point, Centre Island or Ward's Island. From mid-October to April, ferry schedules are restricted, but even at minimum winter service, ferries run hourly to Ward's.

## 8 Tommy Thompson Park

This landfill stretches 4.8 kilometres out to a lighthouse. There are few amenities and it can be very cold in winter. There are huge colonies of Ring-billed Gulls and Double-crested Cormorants. Spotted Sandpipers may be found along the shoreline. In recent years, Canvasbacks have nested in a small pond two kilometres out. Nearby, Ashbridge's Bay Park can also be good. When driving from the city centre, go east on the Gardiner Expressway to Leslie Street, then turn south. A bus runs every half-hour part of the way to the park from May 24 to Thanksgiving. The best fields and marshes are at the base.

## 9 Bluffer's Park

This is another landfill area, which often harbours waterfowl and shorebirds on the lake or in the park's ponds. It gives a good view of the spectacular cliffs, which may hold Peregrine Falcons and Bank Swallows. From Highway 401, head south on McCowan Road at Kingston Road going southwest to Brimley Road, then south on Brimley into the park.

## 10 East Point Park

This is another area where thousands of truckloads of landfill have been converted into an attractive park. However, there are no wilderness areas as at Leslie Spit (Tommy Thompson Park). East Point Park has flocks of ducks in winter and attracts shorebirds around the big pond at its centre. The nearby cliffs may hold Peregrine Falcons, and raptors can be seen at times in migration. From Highway 401, go south on Meadowvale Road to Lawrence Avenue East. Next, go right (west), then first left, and follow its turns into the park.

## 11 Rouge Beach Park

The Rouge River flows through here, creating a marsh and ponds along its length. There are many trails in this very large park, but the best one is at the mouth, on the east side of the river. Cliff Swallows nest under the bridge. The marsh may harbour rails and Common Yellowthroat. Parking is best on the west side of Rouge Beach. From Highway 401, exit at Union Road, go south on Union to Fanfare Avenue, then left (east) until it becomes Ridgewood Road. Follow Ridgewood to where it ends at the lake.

## 12 Frenchman's Bay

Frenchman's Bay has extensive yacht clubs close to Lake Ontario, but the north end is still in a state of wilderness. The area can be excellent for shorebirds in August and September. You will also see waterfowl, and the small woods often hold migrants. Exit Highway 401 at White's Road, then go south 0.3 kilometres, then left on Bayly Street. Go east 1.8 kilometres to a community centre on the lakeside and park here in the southeast corner. Walk east on the trail. Rubber boots are advisable.

## 13 Hydro Park

This park has migrants in spring and fall, a marsh for shorebirds and ducks and a view of the lake at the Pickering Nuclear Station. Since one can only exit Highway 401 at Liverpool Road when driving eastbound, it is necessary to exit at Brock Road. Then go all the way south to Montgomery Park. Head west 0.8 kilometres to Sandy Beach Road, then north 0.5 kilometres to a parking lot on the west side. Walk along the trail through the woods to get to the marsh.

## 14 Squire's Beach

Squire's Beach has vast cattail marshes bordering Duffin Creek. The river broadens into a large pond a few hundred metres before reaching Lake Ontario. This area is also good for shorebirds and even better for waterfowl, as well as Great Blue Herons and Ospreys. Check the bushes for land birds and follow the short trails to the edge of the pond to see the birdlife there. More birds can be seen by going south to the end of Frisco Road, then walking east along the bicycle path. The directions begin the same as for Hydro Park, but at Montgomery Park Road, go east on McKay Road 0.3 kilometres, then angle south-east on Jodrel Road to Montgomery Park Road. Go left here and park near the intersection on the east side.

## 15 Cranberry Marsh

Cranberry Marsh is a large natural pond with cattail marshes around its borders. Of all the birding areas around Toronto, this one is usually the most productive. The large pond holds waterfowl in all seasons, while the forest edges are excellent for migrants. There are two boardwalks that lead to viewing towers on the west side. In September and October, a well-organized hawk watch takes place on the south platform. Days with a few cumulus clouds and a north or northwest wind are best. Nearby Lynde Shores woodlot is a delight for children because the small birds take seeds and nuts right from the hand. Exit Highway 401 at Harwood Road, then drive south to Bayly Street East. Turn left here, passing Regional Road 23. Just past the Ajax-Whitby town line, take Hall's Road on the right.

**16 Thickson Woods**

This small oasis of forest in Oshawa was saved from destruction by fundraising efforts of birders. Migrants are concentrated here, especially in springtime. There are several trails through the woods and a sightings book. For at least two decades, Great Horned Owls have nested here, although one must spend time looking in the pines to find them. To the east are Corbett Creek and a plentiful marsh. The semi-open area to the north has also recently been acquired by naturalists, and trails are being developed. From Highway 401, exit at Thickson Road and go south. Take the second-last left and park here on the road.

**17 Second Marsh**

There is a small lake at the centre of Second Marsh. On the north is an extensive woodland, with well-developed trails and a viewing tower. On the east, after parking in the General Motors (GM) parking lot, visit another viewing tower, then walk the trail down to Lake Ontario. In fall, the west side often has extensive mudflats, attracting hundreds of shorebirds. Among the many gulls are often some Great Black-backed. Ducks may include any of the species in this book. Exit Highway 401 at Harmony Road, then go south to Colonel Sam Drive, then east. Visit the woodland trail, which begins just west of the bridge, before continuing to GM.

**18 Cedarvale Ravine**

This mid-city ravine has been adversely affected in recent years by the erection of apartment buildings. There are some cattail marsh areas and some dry pine forest, as well as numerous bird feeders, which attract winter birds behind the houses at the tops of the hills. These birds may include finches, woodpeckers, nuthatches, cardinals and others. The ravine begins at the north entrance to the St. Clair West subway station and continues northwest. It can also be reached by driving to Bathurst Street and St. Clair Avenue, then north one block, then right (east) to the subway exit. Another ravine continues southeast on the south side of St. Clair.

## 19 Lambton Woods

Much of this area consists of manicured lawn, which has few birds, but the wet woods here are fairly extensive. Of the many good birding areas along the Humber River, none is better than Lambton Woods. There are ducks and gulls on the river, and landbirds, including the Red-bellied Woodpecker. Several feeders attract small birds, many of which will take seeds from the hand. Eastern Screech-Owls are common here, although difficult to find in the day. To get here, go south from Eglinton Avenue on Scarlett Road for 0.3 kilometres to Edenbridge Drive. Turn right (west), drive for 1.1 kilometres and enter the James Gardens parking lot. Walk south from here.

## 20 Wilket Creek and Sunnybrook Parks

This is an area of widespread pine and deciduous forest on both sides of the Don River. Spring is the best time to visit, as the parks become congested with picnickers in summer. Belted Kingfishers can be found along the river. The woods can be good for finches, waxwings, Eastern Screech-Owls and many other species. From Eglinton Road and Leslie Street, go 0.2 kilometres north, then left into the park. The roads and trails extend for 1.5 kilometres to the north and northwest.

## 21 Clairville Conservation Area

This area comprises woodlands and fields, as well as a big reservoir. This area can be good for small owls and hawks in winter. Field birds like Savannah Sparrows are common. To reach the best section, go to the intersection of Highways 50 and 27, then west on 50. After the road has curved to the north, you will see a little gate and a road leading west. Follow this road to a creek valley surrounded by bushes and trees.

## 22 Claremont Conservation Area

This is an extensive woodland with a creek flowing through the centre. This is one of the few locations near Toronto where Ruffed Grouse can be seen. In winter, the whole area is good for northern finches like the Evening Grosbeak. The west border has many multiflora bushes that attract Cedar Waxwings. To reach Claremont, exit Highway 401 at Westney Road, then go north past Highway 7 to the 7th concession. Turn left here and look for the parking lot on the right.

**㉓ Palgrave Conservation Area**

This is an excellent area for birds, especially in winter. There are fields, extensive forests, cedar bogs and ponds. Wild Turkeys can be found here, or at feeders in winter a little farther west, especially along Centreville Creek Avenue. This is a good place to find Sharp-shinned Hawks, Black and White Warblers, Golden-crowned Kinglets and many other birds. Go north on Highway 50 to Patterson Sideroad, which you will see just before reaching the town of Palgrave. Turn left after Bolton, at the next intersection, then turn right to see the extensive woods.

**㉔ Kortright Centre for Conservation**

This area holds open fields and woods. Staff members lead guided nature walks, including "owl prowls." The diverse flora north of the buildings is good for American Robins, Northern Cardinals and Gray Catbirds. There is a daily entrance fee. For information, call 416-667-6299. Drive north on Highway 400 to Major Mackenzie Drive, then left (west). Go past Weston Road to Pine Valley Drive and turn left (south). The entrance will be on your right.

**㉕ Humber Arboretum**

The woodlands and fields are immediately west of Humber College. They can be good for migrants in spring and fall and owls in winter. To reach the area, exit Highway 401 at Highway 27 and go north to Humber College Boulevard, which is just before Finch Avenue. Go left (west) here, enter the huge parking area and head for the southwest corner, where the arboretum is located. The trails begin here.

# Contents

# Common Loon
*Gavia immer*

Observation Calendar

J F M A M J J A S O N D

**Male/Female:** *Summer*: Black head and neck with white banded neck ring; thick grey sharp bill; red eyes; white chest and belly; black back and white spotted wings; black feet and legs. *Winter*: Contrasting blacks and whites muted to dark dull brown. In flight: large feet trail behind tail feathers; quick wing beats close to water's surface; takes off from water by running across surface.

*Did you know? Loons can remain underwater for more than 5 minutes. They dive to feed and to avoid danger.*

**Voice:** Drawn out *lou-lou-lou-lou*-like yodelling, often at dusk or dawn.
**Food:** Small fish.
**Nest/Eggs:** Mound built with aquatic plants, mostly on islands. 2 eggs.

# Double-crested Cormorant

*Phalacrocorax auritus*

Size Identification

Beak

Flying

Observation Calendar

J F M A M J J A S O N D

**Male/Female:** Overall black with long tail feathers; bright orange chin and throat patch; feet and legs black. Crest is visible only during courtship. In flight: neck is kinked.

*Did you know? Cormorants are often seen perched on a rock or pier with wings fully extended to dry their feathers.*

Often seen flying extremely high.

Feeding

**Voice:** Call is a variety of grunts and croaks, only at its nest. Elsewhere silent.
**Food:** Small fish.
**Nest/Eggs:** Colonies. Platform built of sticks and twigs lined with leaves and grass, and placed on ground or small tree. 3-5 eggs.

Egg: Actual Size

# Great Blue Heron
*Ardea herodias*

## Size Identification

## Beak

## Flying

**Male/Female:** Overall grey-blue with black crest on top of head; long neck and bill; black patch around eyes and extending down long yellow bill; white head; long grey legs and feet; long feathers extend over wings and base of neck. In flight: neck is kinked; legs extend past tail; constant wing flapping with occasional glide.

## Feeding

**Voice:** Bill makes clacking sound. Call is a harsh *squawk*.
**Food:** Small fish, reptiles, amphibians, crustaceans, birds, aquatic insects.
**Nest/Eggs:** Colonies. Platform of aquatic plants and twigs lined with softer materials such as down and soft grass, placed in tree. 3-7 eggs.

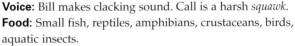

# Turkey Vulture
*Cathartes aura*

Size Identification

Beak

Nesting Location

**Observation Calendar**

J F M A M J J A S O N D

**Male/Female:** Large overall black bird; silver-grey underside of wings is seen in flight; naked red head; pale yellow sharply curved beak; feet and legs charcoal.

*Did you know? Turkey vultures are most commonly seen soaring high over the countryside with their long wings held upward in a wide V-shape.*

**Voice:** Grunts and hisses during aggression or feeding.
**Food:** Carrion.
**Nest/Eggs:** Nest made of scrap on ground, usually in cave, on cliff, hollow of tree or in fallen log. 1-3 eggs.

Vulture

Egg: 60%

# Canada Goose
*Branta canadensis*

**Size Identification**

**Beak**

**Flying**

Observation Calendar

J F M A M J J A S O N D

**Feeding**

**Male/Female:** Black head, neck and bill; white cheek patch; breast and belly pale brown with white flecks; feet and legs black; back and wings brown with white edging; short black tail; white rump, seen in flight. In flight: flies in "V" formations.

**Voice:** Musical *honk*, repeated. Female has slightly higher pitched *honk*.
**Food:** Grass, various seeds and grains.
**Nest/Eggs:** Large nest of twigs, moss and grass lined with down feathers placed near water's edge. 4-8 eggs.

# Mute Swan
*Cygnus olor*

**Size Identification**

**Beak**

**Flying**

Observation Calendar
J F M A M J J A S O N D

**Male/Female:** White overall; bright orange or pink beak; black knob at base of beak; unique S-shaped neck when swimming; feet and legs black.

*Did you know? The Mute Swan, native to Europe, was brought to North America in the nineteenth century as an ornamental species for parks and large estates.*

**Feeding**

**Voice:** Mostly silent. Occasional hissing and barking or loud trumpet call.
**Food:** Fresh and saltwater plants, algae, grains.
**Nest/Eggs:** Large pile of grass and moss lined with feathers, usually built on edge of pond or marsh. 4-6 eggs.

**Egg: 45%**

# Tundra Swan

*Cygnus columbianus*

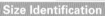

**Size Identification**

**Beak**

**Flying**

Observation Calendar

J F M A M J J A S O N D

**Feeding**

**Male/Female:** Overall white bird; black beak; yellow dash extending from eyes down to base of beak, but not always present; black facial area narrowing to eyes; neck and head occasionally appear lightly rusted colour; feet and legs black.

**Voice:** High-pitched whistling. Bugling sound; *hoo-ho-hoo* when migrating.
**Food:** Aquatic plants, mollusks, grains.
**Nest/Eggs:** Platform built of aquatic plants, grasses and moss on islands. 2-7 eggs.

# Wood Duck
*Aix sponsa*

Observation Calendar

J F M A M J J A S O N D

**Male:** Green head and drooping crest; black cheeks; red eyes and white throat with two spurs; bill orange with black markings; chest brown with white spots leading to white belly; black and green back; sides tan with white and black band. In flight: long squared tail.

**Female:** Back and crown brown; white eye-ring; speckled breast and lighter coloured belly.

**Voice:** Male — high-pitched whistle. Female — loud *oooooeeek* in flight.

**Food:** Aquatic plants, insects, minnows, amphibians.

**Nest/Eggs:** In cavity of tree, as high as 20 metres, or in a log or built structure lined with wood chips and feathers. 9-12 eggs.

# Gadwall

*Anas strepera*

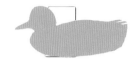

**Size Identification**

**Beak**

**Flying**

**Observation Calendar**

J F M A M J J A S O N D

**Male:** Body over all grey-brown; black rump and tail feathers; light grey pointed feathers on back; feet and legs orange; thin black banding over entire body; black bill.

**Female:** Dull greyish brown and black overall; black bill with orange on sides.

**Feeding**

**Voice:** Quacking and high-pitched descending note from female. Male gives whistle and *rab rab* call.

**Food:** Seeds and aquatic plants.

**Nest/Eggs:** Nest built on islands from plant material and lined with down, slightly concealed. 7-13 eggs.

# American Wigeon
*Anas americana*

Beak

Flying

**Observation Calendar**
J F M A M J J A S O N D

**Male:** White patch running up forehead from bill; green around eyes broadening at cheeks and descending on neck; brown changing to black on back and pointed wings; pointed tail feathers are black with white lines; bill white with black patches on top and on tip. In flight: green on trailing edge of wing; white forewing and belly.
**Female:** Overall light brown with brighter colour running down sides. No green patch on eyes.

Feeding

*Did you know? The American Wigeon is an opportunist: waiting for other diving ducks to come to the surface with their catch, they will attempt to steal the food.*

**Voice:** Male — occasional distinctive whistle: *wh-wh-whew.* Female quacks.
**Food:** Aquatic plants.
**Nest/Eggs:** Grasses lined with down, concealed under brush or tree, a distance from the water. 9-12 eggs.

Egg: 90%

# American Black Duck
*Anas rubripes*

**Size Identification**

**Beak**

**Flying**

Observation Calendar
J F M A M J J A S O N D

**Male:** Dark black with hint of brown overall and blue speculum; bill is olive; feet and legs orange. In flight: white patches at base of wings.
**Female:** Overall lighter brown than male with orange and black bill.

**Voice:** Both female and male *quack*. Male also whistles.
**Food:** Vegetation, insects, amphibians, snails, seeds, grains, berries.
**Nest/Eggs:** Depression on ground lined with grass, leaves and down, close to water's edge. 8-12 eggs.

**Feeding**

# Mallard

*Anas platyrhynchos*

Beak

Flying

J F M A M J J A S O N D

**Male:** Bright green iridescent head, yellow bill; thin white collar; chestnut brown chest; grey sides; black and grey back; white tail; black curled feathers over rump; feet and legs orange. In flight: blue speculum with white border; underparts of wings grey and brown.

**Female:** Overall brown streaked with orange bill, black patches on bill; white tail feathers.

Feeding

**Voice:** Male — call is a soft *raeb* repeated. Female — loud *quacks* repeated.

**Food:** Aquatic plants, grains, insects.

**Nest/Eggs:** Shallow cup built of grasses and aquatic plants lined with feathers on ground concealed near water. 8-10 eggs.

29

Egg: Actual Size

# Blue-winged Teal
*Anas discors*

**Size Identification**

**Beak**

**Flying**

Observation Calendar
J F M A M J J A S O N D

**Male:** Grey head with crescent shaped white patch running up face, black bill; brown chest and belly; back and wings dark brown with buff highlights; blue speculum; yellow feet and legs.
**Female:** Overall brown speckled with pale blue speculum.

**Voice:** Male has high-pitched *peeeep*. Female — *quack* is soft and high-pitched.
**Food:** Aquatic plants, seeds.
**Nest/Eggs:** Pile of grasses lined with down, close to waters edge, concealed. 9-12 eggs.

**Feeding**

# Northern Pintail

*Anas acuta*

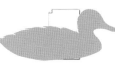

Beak

J F M A M J J A S O N D

Flying

**Male:** Brown head with white line circling around cheeks to chest; white chest and belly; back and wings are black and grey; long tail is black and brown; rump black; sides grey with thin black banding; bill grey with white line. In flight: long tail; white neck and line running up neck.
**Female:** Overall brown with black bill; less pintail feature.

**Voice:** Male has 2 high-pitched whistles. Female quacks.
**Food:** Aquatic plants, seeds, crustaceans, corn, grains.
**Nest/Eggs:** Bowl of sticks, twigs, grasses and lined with down at a distance from water's edge. 6-9 eggs.

Feeding

Egg: 90%

# Green-winged Teal
*Anas crecca*

**Size Identification**

**Beak**

**Flying**

**Observation Calendar**

J F M A M J J A S O N D

**Male:** Head is rust with green patch running around eyes to back of head, black bill, black at back of base of neck; warm grey body with thin black banding; distinctive white bar running down side just in front of wing; white rump; short square tail.

**Female:** Overall dull brown with green speculum; dark band running through eyes.

**Feeding**

**Voice:** Male — high-pitched whistle. Female — weak shrill voice.

**Food:** Seeds, aquatic plants, corn, wheat, oats.

**Nest/Eggs:** On ground, cup shaped, filled with grasses and weeds, sometimes a distance from water. 10-12 eggs.

**Egg: Actual Size**    32

# Ring-necked Duck
*Aythya collaris*

Beak

Flying

Observation Calendar

J F M A M J J A S O N D

**Male:** Back, head and breast black, high forehead; black bill with white outlines; yellow eyes; white spur on breast leading to grey underside and belly. In flight: grey trailing edge; white belly.

**Female:** Grey cheeks and bill; one white band at tip of bill; white eye-ring; dark charcoal back; brown chest, belly and sides.

Feeding

**Voice:** Male has low, loud whistle. Female call is soft *prrrrrrrr* notes. Mostly quiet.

**Food:** Aquatic plants, molluscs, insects.

**Nest/Eggs:** Cup shaped, built of grasses and moss and lined with down feathers, concealed near pond. 8-12 eggs.

33

Egg: 90%

# Bufflehead

*Bucephala albeola*

## Size Identification

## Beak

## Flying

Observation Calendar

J F M A M J J A S O N D

**Male:** Small compact duck; black head with large white patch behind each eye, grey bill; black back with white underparts. **Female:** Grey-brown overall with smaller white patch behind each eye.

**Voice:** Mostly quiet. Male squeals. Female, low *prk prrk*. **Food:** Small fish, crustaceans, molluscs and snails.

## Feeding

# Hooded Merganser
*Lophodytes cucullatus*

Beak

Flying

Observation Calendar
J F M A M J J A S O N D

**Male:** Black crested head with large white patch on back of head behind each eye; black bill is long and thin; rust-coloured eyes; black back with rust sides and white underparts; black band runs down side into chest; white bands on black wings; tail is often cocked. In flight: rapid energetic wing beats.
**Female:** Grey breast and belly; faint rust colour on back of crest; wings dark brown.

Feeding

**Voice:** Call is a low croaking or *gack*.
**Food:** Small fish, reptiles, crustaceans, molluscs and aquatic insects.
**Nest/Eggs:** In tree cavity or built structure lined with grasses and down feathers, occasionally on ground. 9-12 eggs.

Egg: Actual Size

# Common Merganser
*Mergus merganser*

**Size Identification**

**Beak**

**Flying**

**Feeding**

**Observation Calendar**

J F M A M J J A S O N D

**Male:** Dark green head crested with red toothed bill slightly hooked at end; white ring around neck connects to white chest and belly; black back and white sides; feet and legs orange.
**Female:** Brown head and grey-brown back; white chin.

**Voice:** Male call is *twaang*. Female call is series of hard notes.
**Food:** Small fish, crustaceans and molluscs.
**Nest/Eggs:** Built of reeds and grass and lined with down feathers in tree cavity, rock crevice, on ground or in built structure. 8-11 eggs.

# Ruddy Duck
*Oxyura jamaicensis*

Size Identification

Beak

Flying

Observation Calendar
J F M A M J J A S O N D

**Male:** Distinct broad light blue bill; black cap running down back of neck; white cheeks; reddish-brown body; long black tail that is often held upright.
**Female:** Overall brown with white cheeks; buff line just below eyes; beak is black.

**Voice:** Mostly quiet except for drumming and clicking sounds by male during courting.
**Food:** Aquatic plants, crustaceans and aquatic insects.
**Nest/Eggs:** Floating nest of dry plant material lined with down and hidden amongst reeds. 6-20 eggs.

Feeding

Egg: Actual Size

# Osprey
### *Pandion haliaeetus*

**Size Identification**

**Beak**

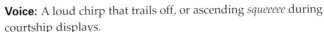

Observation Calendar

J F M A M J J A S O N D

**Nesting Location**

**Male/Female:** In flight: white belly and chest; wings grey with black banding; white wing underparts connect to chest; black band running through eyes; large black bill; tail grey with black banding. Perched: black back and wings with thin white line running above wing; eyes yellow with black band running through and down to cheek; chin white; top of head white with black patches.
**Female:** Larger with a pronounced dark necklace.

**Voice:** A loud chirp that trails off, or ascending *squeeeee* during courtship displays.
**Food:** Various small fish.
**Nest/Eggs:** Constructed of twigs and sticks, lined with sod, grass and vines in upper parts of trees and on top of poles, 60 feet above ground. 2-3 eggs.

**Egg: 65%**          38

# Bald Eagle

*Haliaeetus leucocephalus*

Size Identification

Beak

Observation Calendar
J F M A M J J A S O N D

**Male/Female:** In flight: broad black wings and belly with white head and tail feathers. Perched: white head with brilliant yellow eyes, white tail feathers, black back and wings, yellow feet and legs; yellow bill.

**Juvenile:** Mistaken for Golden Eagle because it lacks white head and tail; chest, white and speckled; black wings with white speckles; underparts black with large areas of white.

*Did you know? The eagle population is now recovering from rapid declines in the 1970s due to the widespread use of DDT and other insecticides.*

Nesting Location

**Voice:** A loud scream given in multiples.

**Food:** A variety of small and medium-sized mammals, fish and carrion.

**Nest/Eggs:** Upper parts of large, often dead, trees built with large twigs, lined with grass, moss, sod and weeds. 2 eggs.

Egg: 70%

**Size Identification**

**Beak**

**Backyard Feeder**

# Sharp-shinned Hawk
*Accipiter striatus*

Observation Calendar
J F M A M J J A S O N D

**Male/Female:** In flight: small hawk with rust-coloured chest banded with buff; long square tail is white with charcoal banding; wings dark brown and rounded; top of head dark brown. Perched: brick-red eyes with brown band just below eye; bill is black with yellow base; feet and legs yellow; white feathers extend out of rust-coloured belly.

*Did you know? Over the past few years there has been a dramatic decrease in the eastern population. This may be directly related to the decrease in songbirds that it hunts.*

**Nesting Location**

**Voice:** A quick high-pitched *kik kik kik*.
**Food:** Small songbirds.
**Nest/Eggs:** Broad platforms of twigs and sticks in conifers or deciduous trees built against the trunk, lined with bark. 4-5 eggs.

# Red-tailed Hawk

*Buteo jamaicensis*

Size Identification

Beak

Observation Calendar
J F M A M J J A S O N D

**Male/Female:** In flight: Tail will appear faint red depending on light; broad wings and belly, white banded with charcoal. Perched: Wings are dark brown with buff edges; eyes brick red; bill yellow and black; feet and legs yellow with white feathers banded brown/charcoal to knees; tail brick red.

**Voice:** A scream that is a downward *keeer er er.*
**Food:** Small mammals, amphibians, nestlings, insects, reptiles and birds.
**Nest/Eggs:** Flat and shallow, stick and twig nest, lined with moss and evergreen sprigs, on rocky ledges or in trees that are in the open, 10-30 metres above ground. 2 eggs.

Nesting Location

Egg: 70%

# Rough-legged Hawk

*Buteo lagopus*

**Size Identification**

**Beak**

Observation Calendar
J F M A M J J A S O N D

**Male/Female:** In-flight: Dark patches on white belly with banding; black patch at wrist of underwing; white tail with one dark band at tip. Perched: Dark brown wings with buff head that is banded with dark brown; yellow eyes; base of tail white rump; black bill, yellow at base; yellow feet and legs with buff feathers that are banded brown to knees.

**Voice:** A whistle along with a *keeeerrr* that descends.
**Food:** Small rodents.
**Nest/Eggs:** Stick nest in tree. 2-4 eggs

**Nesting Location**

# American Kestrel
*Falco sparverius*

Size Identification

Beak

Observation Calendar
J F M A M J J A S O N D

**Male/Female:** In flight: overall buff with black speckles; distinctive black banding on face. Perched: blue-grey wings with black, separated banding; back rust with black banding; grey top of head with rust patch on top; black bands running down cheeks against white; bill black/charcoal with yellow at base; feet and legs orange; tail deep rust with broad black tip.

**Voice:** Rapid *klee klee klee* or *kily kily kily.*
**Food:** Mice, voles, insects and small birds.
**Nest/Eggs:** In cavity of tree or man-made boxes, little or no nesting material. 3-5 eggs.

Birdhouse Nester

Nesting Location

43    Egg: Actual Size

# Peregrine Falcon
*Falco peregrinus*

**Size Identification**

**Beak**

Observation Calendar

J F M A M J J A S O N D

**Male/Female:** In flight: Overall white underside with charcoal banding; face has black mask and sideburns with yellow around dark eyes, bill is yellow and grey, feet and legs are yellow. Perched: Dark grey wings with buff edging on feathers.

*Did you know? The Peregrine falcon has been introduced into large cities where they can nest on top of high-rise buildings.*

**Nesting Location**

**Voice:** A series of high-pitched screams — *ki ki ki.*
**Food:** Catches birds in flight and occasionally will eat larger insects.
**Nest/Eggs:** Slight hollow in rock ledge or flat roof top, built with sticks. 3-5 eggs.

# Ring-necked Pheasant
*Phasianus colchicus*

**Beak**

J F M A M J J A S O N D

**Male:** Green iridescent head with distinctive red wattles (patches around eyes), white collar, overall body is mixture of grey, black and brown; long tail feathers brown with black banding; feet and legs charcoal grey; pale yellow bill.
**Female:** Grey-brown overall with dark markers over entire body; pale yellow bill; small red wattle above eyes.

*Did you know? This chicken-like bird gets into some real cock fights in early spring — jumping, pecking, clawing for their right to territory.*

**Voice:** Loud, harsh *uurk-rk*.
**Food:** Seeds, insects, grains and berries.
**Nest/Eggs:** Shallow bowl on ground lined with weed, grass and leaves. 6-15 eggs.

**Nesting Location**

**Egg: 80%**

# Ruffed Grouse

*Bonasa umbellus*

**Size Identification**

**Beak**

Observation Calendar

J F M A M J J A S O N D

**Male:** Distinctive crest on head; overall brown speckled bird with black shoulder band on back of neck; tail is grey with broad black band at tip; eyes brown; feet and legs grey.
**Female:** Similar to male except browner and more barring on underside; black shoulder band is narrower.

*Did you know? The female will act injured if there is a threat near the nest.*

**Nesting Location**

**Voice:** An alarm note of *qit qit*. Cooing by female. Male does drumming with wings like a distant motorboat.
**Food:** A variety of insects, seeds, tree buds, leaves and berries.
**Nest/Eggs:** Hollow under log or near the base of a tree lined with leaves, pine needles and feathers. 9-12 eggs.

# Wild Turkey

*Meleagris gallopavo*

Beak

**Observation Calendar**

J F M A M J J A S O N D

**Male:** An extremely large bird, overall dark dusky-brown body; iridescent bronze sheen and banding of reddish-brown, black and white; head is featherless, grey and red; blueish and reddish wattles; tail is fan shaped when open and has chestnut or buff tips; spurs and 'beard' on breast; feet and legs reddish-grey.

**Female:** Smaller than male and less iridescence; no spurs or 'beard.'

**Voice:** Gobbling and clucking calls.

**Food:** Seeds, grains, insects, frogs, lizards, vegetation and nuts.

**Nest/Eggs:** Scraped depression in ground lined with leaves and grasses. 6-20 eggs.

Nesting Location

47

Egg: 65%

# Virginia Rail

*Rallus limicola*

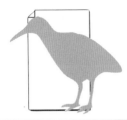

**Size Identification**

**Beak**

**Flying**

**Feeding**

Observation Calendar
J F M A M J J A S O N D

**Male/Female:** Chicken-like; grey head banded dark charcoal on top; eyes red; neck and sides rich rust; long curved red and black bill; back dark brown with rust edging; wings rust with black; short brown tail; legs and feet red; belly black and white banding.

**Voice:** Call is a *kicket* repeated with grunting notes.
**Food:** Marine worms, snails, aquatic insects.
**Nest/Eggs:** Cup built of grass and reeds built slightly above water's surface attached to reeds and other aquatic plant life. 5-12 eggs.

# Sora
*Porzana carolina*

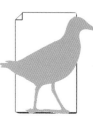

Beak

Flying

Observation Calendar

J F M A M J J A S O N D

**Male/Female:** Chicken-like; grey colouring above eyes runs down to chin, breast and belly; black mask behind thick yellow bill; upper parts chestnut brown with white and dark brown bars; legs and feet yellow.

*Did you know? The Sora, like other rails, prefers to migrate at night.*

Feeding

**Voice:** Call is a musical *kuur weeee*, which is repeated and descends.
**Food:** Aquatic insects and seeds.
**Nest/Eggs:** Built in open marsh, attached to reeds, using leaves and grass. 6-15 eggs.

49  Egg: Actual Size

# American Coot

*Fulica americana*

**Size Identification**

**Beak**

**Flying**

Observation Calendar
J F M A M J J A S O N D

**Male/Female:** Duck-like body, slate-coloured overall; white bill and frontal shield shows red swelling at close range; partial black ring around tip of beak; feet and legs greenish-yellow; lobed toes.

*Did you know? The American Coot has many different courtship displays, including running over the surface of water with its neck and head bent very low.*

**Feeding**

**Voice:** Variety of calls including clucks, grunts and other harsh notes and toots sounding like a small trumpet.
**Food:** Seeds, leaves, roots and small aquatic plants.
**Nest/Eggs:** Floating platform nest of dead leaves and stems lined with finer material and anchored to reeds. 8-10 eggs.

**Egg: Actual Size**    50

# Killdeer
*Charadrius vociferus*

**Size Identification**

**Beak**

**Flying**

J F M A M J J A S O N D

**Male/Female:** Bright red eyes with black band running across forehead; white chin, collar and eyebrow; black collar ring under white; black chest band set against white chest and belly; back and wings rust and grey; wing tipped in black; legs and feet pink/grey. In flight: orange rump; black wing tips and white band through center.

**Feeding**

*Did you know? A Killdeer will exhibit a "broken-wing" display when a predator comes close to the nest site. The bird will appear hurt and run around distracting the predator from the nest.*

**Voice:** Variety of calls with most common being *kill deeee,* which is repeated.
**Food:** Insects.
**Nest/Eggs:** Hollow on ground with some pebbles. Most popular sightings in gravel parking lots. 3-4 eggs.

**Egg: Actual Size**

# Spotted Sandpiper
*Actitis macularia*

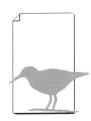

**Size Identification**

**Beak**

**Flying**

Observation Calendar
J F M A M J J A S O N D

**Male/Female:** *Summer*: Grey-brown on head, back and wings; white eyebrow and black line running from beak to back of neck; long orange bill; white chin, chest and belly with distinct charcoal spots; yellow feet and legs; bobbing tail.
*Winter*: White underparts — no spots. In flight: quick stiff wingbeats, slightly arched back.

**Feeding**

**Voice:** Quiet bird but makes a *peeetaawet* call during courtship and a whistle that is repeated when alarmed.
**Food:** Insects, worms, crustaceans, fish, flies and beetles.
**Nest/Eggs:** Shallow depression on ground lined with grasses and mosses. 4 eggs.

# Ring-billed Gull
*Larus delawarensis*

Beak

Flying

J F M A M J J A S O N D

**Male/Female:** *Summer*: White overall; yellow bill with black band at end; yellow eyes; pale grey wings and black tips and white patches within black tips; yellow feet and legs. *Winter*: Feet and legs turn paler; light brown spots on top of head and back of neck. In flight: grey underparts; black wing tips.

**Voice:** Loud *kaawk* and other calls.
**Food:** Dives for fish, also eats insects, bird eggs, worms, garbage.
**Nest/Eggs:** Colonies. Grasses, sticks, twigs and pebbles built on ground. 3 eggs.

Feeding

53    Egg: Actual Size

# Herring Gull
*Larus argentatus*

Observation Calendar

J F M A M J J A S O N D

**Male/Female:** White head that in winter is streaked light brown; yellow eyes and bill; small red patch on lower bill; tail black; feet and legs pink. In flight: grey wing with white on trailing edge and black tips; pale brown rump; wide charcoal tail feathers.

**Voice:** Variety of squawks and squeals. Aggressive alarm call is *kak kak kak kak* ending in *yucca*.
**Food:** Insects, small mammals, clams, fish, small birds, crustaceans, mussels, rodents, garbage.
**Nest/Eggs:** Colonies. Mound lined with grass and seaweed on ground or cliff. Usually on islands. 2-4 eggs.

# Great Black-backed Gull

*Larus marinus*

Beak

Flying

Observation Calendar

J F M A M J J A S O N D

Feeding

**Male/Female:** White head, chin, chest and belly, red patch on lower portion of bill; feet and legs pink/grey; black wings with thin white band on trailing edge; tail and back black. In flight: pale grey undersides with black wing tip; tail white.

**Voice:** Loud squawks and deep guttural notes.
**Food:** Scavenger. Small fish, mammals, young birds and garbage. Major predator of other birds including puffin and tern chicks.
**Nest/Eggs:** Colonies. Mound of seaweed and other coastal plants lined with grasses on ground or rocky ledge. 3 eggs.

Egg: 80%

# Rock Dove (Pigeon)
*Columba livia*

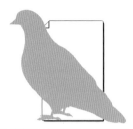

**Size Identification**

**Beak**

**Backyard Feeder**

Observation Calendar
J F M A M J J A S O N D

**Male/Female:** Varies greatly from solid white to solid black and everything in between. Most birds have dark grey head with hints of iridescent colours along the neck; body light grey with two charcoal wing bands; tail and wings dark grey with black bands; rump is white.

*Did you know? Pigeons were introduced to North America in the 1800s. They are now common everywhere, especially in urban areas.*

**Voice:** Soft descending *kooooo kooooo*.
**Food:** Seeds and grains.
**Nest/Eggs:** Flimsy nest of twigs, grass, straw and debris, on ledges or crevices of buildings and bridges, in colonies. 1-2 eggs.

**Nesting Location**

**Egg: Actual Size** 56

# Mourning Dove
*Zenaida macroura*

**Size Identification**

**Beak**

**Backyard Feeder**

Observation Calendar

J F M A M J J A S O N D

**Male:** Buff-coloured head and body; dark grey wings and tail; bill is black with speckles of red at opening; wings have small black feathers highlighted against softer grey; eyes black surrounded by light blue; feet and legs red; tail is long and pointed.
**Female:** Similar except for head, neck and chest, which are evenly brown.

*Did you know? When the Mourning Dove is in flight its wings whistle.*

**Voice:** Very distinct cooing that sounds a little sad, *coooahooo-oo -oo-oo* fading at the end.
**Food:** A variety of seeds and grains.
**Nest/Eggs:** Platform of sticks and twigs, lined with grass and rootlets, in evergreens, up to 15 metres above ground. 1-2 eggs.

**Nesting Location**

57 **Egg: Actual Size**

# Black-billed Cuckoo

*Coccyzus erythropthalmus*

**Size Identification**

**Beak**

Observation Calendar

J F M A M J J A S O N D

**Male/Female:** Distinct black beak curved slightly downward; red ring around black eyes; upper body parts brown; wings brown; long tail with 3 white spots on underside; white chin, chest and belly; feet and legs charcoal grey.

*Did you know? The Black-billed Cuckoo is an important species for farmers since much of its diet consists of caterpillars, which are destructive to plants.*

**Nesting Location**

**Voice:** Softly repeated *cu cu cu cu cu* in groups of 2-5 at the same pitch.
**Food:** Insects, lizards, mollusks, fishes, frogs and berries.
**Nest/Eggs:** Shallow, built of twigs and grasses and lined with softer materials including ferns, roots and plant-down; usually built near tree trunk in dense area. 2-5 eggs.

**Egg: Actual Size** 58

# Yellow-billed Cuckoo

*Coccyzus americanus*

Beak

Observation Calendar

J F M A M J J A S O N D

**Male/Female:** Overall brownish grey on upper parts; long curved black beak with yellow below; long black tail with 3 white ovals on underside; white chin, chest and belly; feet and legs black.

**Voice:** Call is a rapid *ka ka ka ka kow kow kowp kowp*, slowing down at end.

**Food:** Hairy caterpillar and other insects, berries, frogs and lizards.

**Nest/Eggs:** Flimsy saucer built of twigs and lined with leaves and grasses, built in bushes or small trees. 1-4 eggs.

Nesting Location

Egg: Actual Size

# Eastern Screech-Owl

*Otus asio*

**Size Identification**

**Beak**

**Birdhouse Nester**

**Nesting Location**

Observation Calendar

J F M A M J J A S O N D

**Male/Female:** Small reddish or brown-grey owl with mottling of dark brown; large yellow eyes; feet and legs pale; small black curved beak; reddish ear tufts. Also occurs in grey morph with grey intermediates.

**Voice:** Call is high-pitched rising and lowering with long trill. Soft purring and trills.
**Food:** Mice, insects, amphibians, small birds.
**Nest/Eggs:** Tree cavity with no lining added. 3-6 eggs.

# Great Horned Owl
*Bubo virginianus*

Beak

Observation Calendar

J F M A M J J A S O N D

**Male/Female:** Very recognizable ear tufts that sit wide apart; bright yellow eyes surrounded by rust colour; grey and brown overall with black bands.

**Voice:** Hoot consists of *hoo hoo hoo hoo hoo hoo*.
**Food:** Small mammals, birds and reptiles.
**Nest/Eggs:** Nests in a deserted hawk's, heron's or crow's nest with very little material added. Occasionally will lay eggs on ground amongst bones, skulls and bits of fur. 1-3 eggs.

Nesting Location

Egg: 70%

# Chimney Swift

*Chaetura pelagica*

**Size Identification**

**Beak**

**Observation Calendar**
J F M A M J J A S O N D

**Male/Female:** Dark charcoal on head, back, wings and tail; lighter on chest and throat; black bill is small with light grey on underside; feet and legs grey.

*Did you know? A Chimney Swift is capable of snapping off tree twigs with its feet while in flight. It then takes the twig in its mouth and returns to its nest.*

**Nesting Location**

**Voice:** A very quick and repeated *chitter, chitter, chitter* with occasional *chip.*

**Food:** Flying insects such as moths and beetles.

**Nest/Eggs:** Flimsy half-cup attached by saliva to crevice or ledge in chimneys, barns and old buildings, and on rock formations. 3-6 eggs.

# Ruby-throated Hummingbird
*Archilochus colubris*

Beak

Backyard Feeder

Observation Calendar
J F M A M J J A S O N D

**Male:** Dark green head that is iridescent in parts; red throat, darker under chin; white collar, breast and belly; wings and notched tail black; iridescent green on back; black bill is long and thin; feet and legs black.

**Female:** Head, back and parts of tail are bright iridescent green; white throat, chest and belly; wings and tail black with white outer tips; black bill is long and thin; small white area behind eyes; feet and legs black.

**Voice:** A low *hummmmmm* produced by wings. Occasionally an angry sounding squeak or chattering.

**Food:** Nectar from a variety of plants including thistles, jewelweed, trumpet vines and other blossoms; occasionally insects.

**Nest/Eggs:** Thimble-sized, tightly woven cup with deep cavity built with fibres and attached with spiderweb, lined with plant down, covered on the outside with lichens, in tree or shrub, 3-6 metres above ground. 2 eggs.

Nesting Location

63  Egg: Actual Size

# Belted Kingfisher
*Ceryle alcyon*

**Size Identification**

**Beak**

**Flying**

Observation Calendar

J F M A M J J A S O N D

**Feeding**

**Male:** A large crested blue/black head and long black bill; wings black with white bands; chest white; white collar wraps around neck with blue band that wraps around chest; very short blue tail; feet and legs charcoal.
**Female:** Rust-coloured breast band.

*Did you know? Belted Kingfishers teach their young to dive for food by catching a fish, stunning it, then placing it on the surface of the water. The young birds then practice diving for it.*

**Voice:** A continuous deep rattle during flight.
**Food:** Small fish, amphibians, reptiles, insects and crayfish.
**Nest/Eggs:** A cavity or tunnel excavated in a bank near a river or lake. 5-8 eggs.

**Egg: Actual Size**    64

# Red-headed Woodpecker

*Melanerpes erythrocephalus*

Observation Calendar

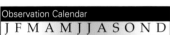
J F M A M J J A S O N D

**Male/Female:** Bright red hood over head with grey and black bill; back is black with large distinctive white patches on wings; feet and legs grey; tail feathers are pointed and black; chest and belly white.

*Did you know? These woodpeckers are declining because of forestry practices and are competing unsuccessfully with European Starlings for nesting locations.*

**Voice:** Call is a deep hoarse *queer queeeer queeer.*
**Food:** A variety of insects and insect larvae.
**Nest/Eggs:** Cavity of tree with no added material, 2-25 metres above ground. 4-7 eggs.

# Red-bellied Woodpecker

*Melanerpes carolinus*

**Size Identification**

**Beak**

**Backyard Feeder**

**Birdhouse Nester**

**Nesting Location**

**Egg: Actual Size**

Observation Calendar

J F M A M J J A S O N D

**Male:** Bright red cap stretching down back of neck; long sharp black beak; tan chin, chest and belly; short black tail with white stripes; black back with white bands; feet and legs charcoal grey; reddish patch on lower belly seldom visible.
**Female:** Grey face with red crown running down back of head.

*Did you know? The Red-bellied Woodpecker will store food in tree cavities and crevices.*

**Voice:** Harsh *churrrr* and *chuck chuck chuck* descending in pitch. Drums and bursts.
**Food:** Insects, fruit, seeds and nuts.
**Nest/Eggs:** Creates cavity in living or nearly dead tree. 3-8 eggs.

# Downy Woodpecker

*Picoides pubescens*

Beak

Backyard Feeder

Birdhouse Nester

Nesting Location

Observation Calendar

J F M A M J J A S O N D

**Male:** Black crown ends in very bright red spot on back of head; white extends from cheeks to lower belly; wings and tail black with white banding; feet and legs grey.
**Female:** Similar except without red spot on back of head.

**Voice:** A bright sounding *peek...peek,* which may be followed by a rattling call. Listen for bird pounding on trees looking for insects.
**Food:** Larvae and other tree-dwelling insects.
**Nest/Eggs:** Cavity of tree with no added material, 1-5 metres above ground. 3-6 eggs.

Egg: Actual Size

# Hairy Woodpecker

*Picoides villosus*

**Beak**

**Backyard Feeder**

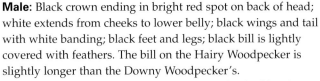

Observation Calendar

J F M A M J J A S O N D

**Male:** Black crown ending in bright red spot on back of head; white extends from cheeks to lower belly; black wings and tail with white banding; black feet and legs; black bill is lightly covered with feathers. The bill on the Hairy Woodpecker is slightly longer than the Downy Woodpecker's.
**Female:** Similar except without red spot on back of head.

*Did you know? An easy way to identify Downy and Hairy Woodpeckers is that they both spread their tails when perched against the side of a tree.*

**Nesting Location**

**Voice:** Hairy Woodpeckers make various sounds as they pound on trees. One sound is for hole digging while another is when it is looking for food.
**Food:** Larvae and other tree-dwelling insects, fruits, ants and corn.
**Nest/Eggs:** Cavity of tree with no added material, up to 10 metres above ground. 3-6 eggs.

# Northern Flicker

*Colaptes auratus*

Size Identification

Beak

Backyard Feeder

J F M A M J J A S O N D

**Male:** Grey at top of head, which stops at bright red spot on back of neck; black eyes are encircled in light brown, with a black line running off bill to lower neck; chest begins with black half-moon necklace on front and turns into a white belly with black spots; wings and tail greyish-brown with black banding; white rump; yellow feathers are evident under sharp pointed tail feathers while in flight.

**Female:** Similar to male except without the black line running from bill.

**Voice:** Various sounds depending on its use. When claiming its territory, a series of *kekekekeke*, and when in courtship, *woeka-woeka-woeka*.

**Food:** Digs and pokes on the ground looking for ants and other insects, fruit and seeds. Most of its diet consists of ants.

**Nest/Eggs:** Cavity of tree with no added material, up to 18 metres above ground. 3-10 eggs.

Nesting Location

69  Egg: Actual Size

# Eastern Wood-Pewee
*Contopus virens*

**Beak**

Observation Calendar
J F M A M J J A S O N D

**Male/Female:** Olive-grey overall with head that is crested at back; wings black and dark grey with two white bars; throat and chest white; belly slightly yellow or white; tail charcoal; bill black on top and yellow underside; feet and legs black.

*Did you know? The Wood-Pewee changes its voice in morning and evening, converting its song into a slow verse.*

**Nesting Location**

**Voice:** A soft whistle, *pee-a-wee pee-awee*, repeated without any pause early in the morning.
**Food:** Flies, beetles, bees, ants and other insects.
**Nest/Eggs:** Shallow cup built with grass, spiderweb and fibres lined with hair, covered outside with lichens, on horizontal branch of tree far out from trunk, 5-20 metres above ground. 3-5 eggs.

# Least Flycatcher
*Empidonax minimus*

Size Identification

Size Identification

Beak

Observation Calendar

J F M A M J J A S O N D

**Male/Female:** Smallest of the flycatchers with a brown/olive head and back; rump is slightly golden; throat white and washes to a grey breast and a pale yellow belly; black eyes are ringed with white; wings dark brown and black with white wing bands; tail dark olive/brown with white edges.

*Did you know? The Least Flycatcher is not afraid of humans, and when it is in pursuit of a flying insect it will dive very close to a person.*

Nesting Location

**Voice:** Song is *chibic chibic chibic* repeated with accent in middle of phrase.
**Food:** Flying insects.
**Nest/Eggs:** Compact and deep cup built with bark, weeds, grasses and lined with thistle, feathers, hair and fibres, in upright fork of tree or shrub, 1-20 metres above ground. 3-6 eggs.

Egg: Actual Size

# Eastern Phoebe
*Sayornis phoebe*

Observation Calendar
J F M A M J J A S O N D

**Male/Female:** Grey-brown head and back with white throat and chest; feet and legs black; white wing bands; pale yellow belly.

*Did you know? One quick way to identify this bird is to watch the greyish brown tail bobbing up and down.*

**Voice:** Song is a rough-sounding *fee bee fee bee.* Call is *wit.*
**Food:** Flying insects as well as ground insects.
**Nest/Eggs:** Large shelf structure built with weeds, grass, fibres and mud, covered with moss, lined with grass and hair. 3-6 eggs.

# Great Crested Flycatcher

*Myiarchus crinitus*

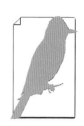

Beak

Observation Calendar

J F M A M J J A S O N D

**Male/Female:** Olive/grey head with crest; back is olive/grey; wings are black with olive/grey edges and rust colour on outer edge; tail strong reddish-brown; throat soft grey changing to pale yellow at belly; feet and legs black.

*Did you know? The Great Crested Flycatcher will sometimes use foil or cellophane in its nest.*

**Voice:** A throaty whistle *wheeep* or a rolling *prrrreeeet*.
**Food:** Flying insects and a variety of ground insects.
**Nest/Eggs:** Bulky cup built with twig, leaves, feather, bark and cast off snakeskin, or cellophane, in natural cavity of tree, up to 18 metres above ground. 4-8 eggs.

Birdhouse Nester

Nesting Location

73   Egg: Actual Size

# Eastern Kingbird

*Tyrannus tyrannus*

**Size Identification**

**Beak**

Observation Calendar

J F M A M J J A S O N D

**Male/Female:** Black head, back, wings and tail; white chin, chest and belly; wings have white along edge and tail has white band along tip; feet and legs black.

*Did you know? Size does not matter to the Eastern Kingbird: they will attack crows, ravens, hawks and owls to defend their territory.*

**Nesting Location**

**Voice:** Several different calls, including *tzi tzee* as a true song. Also a *kitter kitter kitter* when threatened.

**Food:** Flying insects, and fruit in late summer.

**Nest/Eggs:** Bulky cup built with weed stalks, grass and moss, in branches of tree or shrub, 3-6 metres above ground. 3-5 eggs.

# Warbling Vireo
*Vireo gilvus*

Beak

Observation Calendar
J F M A M J J A S O N D

**Male/Female:** Grey and green head, neck and back; white eyebrow extending from black bill; white chin, breast and belly with variable amounts of yellow; feet and legs black; tail and wings slightly darker.

**Voice:** The best way to find a Warbling Vireo is to listen. This bird sings throughout the day with a beautiful warbling sound. Song is group of slurred phrases such as *brig-a-dier brig-a-dier brigate.*

**Food:** Small insects including caterpillars, beetles and moths, and some berries.

**Nest/Eggs:** Tightly woven pensile cup built with bark, leaves, grass, feathers, plant down and spiderweb, lined with stems and horsehair, suspended in tall trees at the edge of wooded area, well away from trunk. 3-5 eggs.

Nesting Location

Egg: Actual Size

# Red-eyed Vireo
*Vireo olivaceus*

**Observation Calendar**

J F M A M J J A S O N D

**Male/Female:** *Spring:* red eyes encircled with thin line of black set against a wide white eyebrow that runs from bill to back of head; black bill; throat and chest white; feet and legs black; back and rump are olive green; wings and tail black with edges of olive green; eyes are darker brown in winter.

**Voice:** The Red-eyed Vireo may sound over 40 different phrases in just 60 seconds, then begin all over again. A variety of short phrases including *cherrrwit chereeee cissy a witt teeeooo.*
**Food:** Small insects, berries and fruit.
**Nest/Eggs:** Deep cup built with grass, paper, bark, rootlets, vine and decorated outside with spiderweb and lichen, suspended in branches, up to 18 metres above ground; 4 eggs.

# Blue Jay

*Cyanocitta cristata*

Size Identification

Beak

Backyard Feeder

Observation Calendar

J F M A M J J A S O N D

**Male/Female:** Bright blue crested head with black band running through eyes to just under crest on back of neck; black band continues along side of neck on both sides to chest; white under chin; back is blue; wings and tail are blue banded with black and tipped with white at ends; black bill is large with light feathers covering nostril area; feet and legs black.

*Did you know? The Blue Jay has a bad reputation for eating the eggs of other birds, and even their young.*

**Voice:** Call is *jay jay jay,* plus many other calls including mimicking hawks.

**Food:** Omnivorous — in summer months the Blue Jay feasts on just about anything, including spiders, snails, salamanders, frogs, seeds and caterpillars. In winter months they supplement their diet with acorns and other nuts stored in tree cavities earlier in the year.

**Nest/Eggs:** Bulky nest of sticks, leaves, string and moss lined with small roots, well hidden, 1-15 metres above ground, in tree or shrub. 4-5 eggs.

Nesting Location

77  Egg: Actual Size

# American Crow
*Corvus brachyrhynchos*

**Size Identification**

**Beak**

**Backyard Feeder**

Observation Calendar
J F M A M J J A S O N D

**Male/Female:** Overall shiny black with a hint of purple in direct sunlight; large broad black bill; short and slightly square tail; feet and legs black.

*Did you know? Although one might think that crows are a nuisance bird, they actually devour large quantities of grasshoppers, beetles and grubs that can be destructive to crops.*

**Voice:** A variety of calls. Most common is the long *caaaaaw*, which softens at the end.
**Food:** Omnivorous — insects, food waste, grains, seeds and carrion.
**Nest/Eggs:** Large basket of twigs, sticks, vines, moss, feathers, fur and hair, on ledge in crotch of tree or shrub. 3-4 eggs.

**Nesting Location**

**Egg: Actual Size** 78

# Horned Lark

*Eremophila alpestris*

Beak

J F M A M J J A S O N D

**Male/Female:** Dull brown on top; chest and belly white; wings and tail brown and black; distinctive black facial marks, which include small horns (feathers) on either side of its head; chin pale yellow with black band above running through eyes and down; feet and legs black.

*Did you know? The horns are not always visible, but a quick way to identify the Horned Lark is that on the ground it walks and does not hop, like most small birds.*

**Voice:** Soft twittering *tsee titi* or *zzeeet*.
**Food:** A variety of insects, seeds and grains.
**Nest/Eggs:** Hollow in ground under grass tuft, made of stems and leaves, lined with grass. 3-5 eggs.

Nesting Location

Egg: Actual Size

# Purple Martin
*Progne subis*

**Beak**

**Birdhouse Nester**

**Nesting Location**

**Observation Calendar**
J F M A M J J A S O N D

**Male:** Very shiny, dark purple overall, with black wings and tail; black bill is short and slightly curved; feet and legs reddish black; wings very long reaching to tip of tail when folded.
**Female:** Dull purple head and back with black wings and tail; chest and chin grey; belly white with black speckles; feet and legs black.

**Voice:** Call is a high-pitched *cheer cheer*.
**Food:** Flying insects.
**Nest/Eggs:** Deep cup in tree cavity lined with grass and leaves, usually in large colonies. Also nests in gourds and special martin houses. 3-8 eggs.

**Egg: Actual Size** 80

# Tree Swallow

*Tachycineta bicolor*

**Beak**

J F M A M J J A S O N D

**Male/Female:** Dark iridescent blue on head, neck, back, wings and tail; bright white chin, chest and belly; black bill is short and slightly curved; wings are very long reaching down to tip of tail when folded; feet and legs charcoal.

**Birdhouse Nester**

*Did you know? The Tree Swallow is the only swallow that eats berries in the place of insects. This allows it to winter further north than its relatives.*

**Voice:** Early morning song *wheet trit weet*, with an alarm call of *cheedeeep.*
**Food:** Flying insects and berries.
**Nest/Eggs:** Cup in cavity of tree lined with grass and feathers, usually a woodpecker's old hole. 4-6 eggs.

**Nesting Location**

**Egg: Actual Size**

# Northern Rough-winged Swallow

*Stelgidopteryx serripennis*

**Size Identification**

**Beak**

Observation Calendar
J F M A M J J A S O N D

**Male/Female:** Greyish pale brown upper parts; pale brown chin, chest and sides; white belly; feet and legs black; short black beak; short tail.

**Voice:** Harsh *brrrrrt* during aggression or danger. Musical *br rrrrt* drawn out and often doubled.
**Food:** Insects in flight.
**Nest/Eggs:** Built in cavities such as tunnels, bridges, culverts and caves, lined with grass, leaves and moss. 4-8 eggs.

**Nesting Location**

# Bank Swallow

*Riparia riparia*

Beak

Observation Calendar

J F M A M J J A S O N D

**Male/Female:** Dirty brown overall with white front except for brown band running across chest; wings are very long, reaching down to tip of tail when folded; feet and legs grey; black bill is short.

**Voice:** A variety of calls including *tchirrt tchirrt* and long twittering.
**Food:** Flying insects as well as a variety of other insects. Main diet consists of dragonflies, flies, mayflies and beetles.
**Nest/Eggs:** Earth tunnel lined with grass and straw along bank near water. 4-6 eggs.

Nesting Location

Egg: Actual Size

# Cliff Swallow
*Petrochelidon pyrrhonota*

Size Identification

Beak

Observation Calendar
J F M A M J J A S O N D

**Male/Female:** Dark grey back and wings with buff rump and brick red cheeks; white patch on forehead; belly white; back has variable amounts of white streaks; feet and legs grey; tail black, square at end.

*Did you know? Nest sites can be a little competitive and the birds will steal nesting grasses and twigs from each other's nests.*

Nesting Location

**Voice:** A long *chuuurrrr* and a deeper *nyeeew*.
**Food:** A variety of insects.
**Nest/Eggs:** Mud lined with grass, hair and feathers, under bridges, in cliffs and buildings. 3-6 eggs.

# Barn Swallow

*Hirundo rustica*

**Beak**

**Observation Calendar**
J F M A M J J A S O N D

**Male:** Dark blue iridescent from top of head, shoulders, down back and top of wings; chin and chest rust colour; wings are very long and extend to tips of tail, which is forked with long outer feathers that can be seen when bird is in flight; feet and legs charcoal; black and cream bill. When bird is in flight a band of white can be seen at end of tail.
**Female:** Same markings but duller.

*Did you know? Barn Swallows are amazing to watch as they skim over water and pick insects off the surface. In the evening they hunt mosquitoes.*

**Nesting Location**

**Voice:** A soft twittering *kvik kvik wit wit*.
**Food:** A variety of insects.
**Nest/Eggs:** Mud and straw lined with feathers, in buildings, under bridges, in cliffs and caves. 4-5 eggs.

**Egg: Actual Size**

# Black-capped Chickadee

*Poecile atricapilla*

Beak

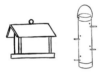

Backyard Feeder

Birdhouse Nester

Nesting Location

Observation Calendar
J F M A M J J A S O N D

**Male/Female:** Round black head with white cheeks; black chin that contrasts against bright white breast, which fades into rust on belly with buff edges; wings black and grey with white edges; tail black with white edges; feet and legs black.

*Did you know? In winter Black-capped Chickadees form small flocks of about 10 birds and defend their territory from intruders.*

**Voice:** A descending whistle with two notes and sounds like *chick-a-dee-dee-dee.*
**Food:** Seeds, insects and berries. Drawn to thistle-seed feeders.
**Nest/Eggs:** Domed cup lined with wool, hair, fur, moss and insect cocoons, in cavity of tree. 5-10 eggs.

# Red-breasted Nuthatch
*Sitta canadensis*

Observation Calendar

J F M A M J J A S O N D

**Male:** Small round bird with black stripe over top of head and white stripe underneath, followed by black band running through eyes; white cheeks turn to rust colour at neck and continue rust to chest and belly; back is grey-blue; wings and tail grey becoming black at ends; black bill is often white on underside; feet and legs brown-black.

**Female:** Similar to male except for grey cap and light underside.

*Did you know? The Red-breasted Nuthatch will smear pitch at the entrance to its nest, although it is not known why.*

**Voice:** A tin-whistle call and an occasional loud *knack knack*.
**Food:** Seeds, insects and flying insects.
**Nest/Eggs:** Cup lined with grass, moss and feathers, in excavated cavity or crevice of tree. 1-12 metres above ground. 4-7 eggs.

# White-breasted Nuthatch
*Sitta carolinensis*

**Size Identification**

**Beak**

**Backyard Feeder**

**Birdhouse Nester**

**Nesting Location**

Observation Calendar
J F M A M J J A S O N D

**Male:** Shiny black on top of head running down the back, turning to lighter blue-grey on back; white face and neck, chest and belly; slight rust colours on sides; wings and tail are blue-grey with white edges; feet and legs black.
**Female:** Similar to male except top of head and back are lighter grey.

*Did you know? These little birds are known for their ability to run down tree trunks headfirst, at a very fast pace.*

**Voice:** Nesting pairs keep in contact with one another with a deep sounding *aank aank* but also chatter a soft *ip ip*.
**Food:** Spiders, insects, seeds, insect eggs and acorns.
**Nest/Eggs:** Cup lined with twig, feathers, small roots, fur and hair, in natural cavity or crevice of tree, 4-15 metres above ground. 5-10 eggs.

# Brown Creeper

*Certhia americana*

Size Identification

Beak

Backyard Feeder

Observation Calendar

J F M A M J J A S O N D

**Male/Female:** Overall brown with grey streaks and white chin, chest and belly; long curved bill that is black on top and white/pink on bottom; distinctive eye stripe; feet and legs grey; tail is long and pointed.

*Did you know? Spending most of its day creeping up and down trees looking for meals, the Brown Creeper can flatten itself and blend into the colour of the tree trunk when a predator passes by.*

**Voice:** A very high whistling *see wee see tu eee.*
**Food:** Insects, insect and spider eggs and occasionally nuts and seeds.
**Nest/Eggs:** Cup with foundation of twig, bark and leaves, lined with bark, grass, feathers and moss, in cavity or under loose bark of tree, up to 5 metres above ground. 4-8 eggs.

Nesting Location

89 Egg: Actual Size

# House Wren

*Troglodytes aedon*

Observation Calendar
J F M A M J J A S O N D

**Male/Female:** Brown upper parts; light buff eyebrows; short rust and black banded tail that is often cocked; light buff chin, chest and belly; light buff banding along sides; feet and legs greyish pink; sharp black beak with yellow lower mandible.

**Voice:** Warbling that descends for 2-3 seconds. Call is a variety of buzzes and rattling *chur*.
**Food:** Insects.
**Nest/Eggs:** In cavities of trees or birdhouses, twigs lined with softer material including moss, feathers, rootlets and grasses. 5-6 eggs.

# Golden-crowned Kinglet
*Regulus satrapa*

Observation Calendar
J F M A M J J A S O N D

**Male:** One of the smallest woodland birds with black head stripes that set off its crown patch of orange; neck and back olive-grey; wings and tail olive with black along edges; feet and legs black; pale grey wingbars; pale eyebrow.
**Female:** Similar to male except patch on top is yellow.

*Did you know? Their movements on a tree make them easy to spot. They flutter their wings as they look for insects.*

**Voice:** Very high pitched, dropping to a quick chatter. The song is so highly pitched that some people cannot hear its song.
**Food:** A variety of insects, spiders, fruits and seeds.
**Nest/Eggs:** Deep cup built with moss and lichen at top, lined with black rootlets and feathers suspended from conifer branch, up to 30 metres above ground. 5-11 eggs.

91

# Ruby-crowned Kinglet

*Regulus calendula*

**Size Identification**

**Beak**

Observation Calendar
J F M A M J J A S O N D

**Male:** Olive-grey overall with white eye-ring broken at top; crested with red patch on head; chin and neck are lighter olive-grey; feet and legs black; wings and tail buff with black edges; white bands on wings.
**Female:** Similar to male except for no red patch on top of head.

*Did you know? The ruby red top on the male is hard to see unless he is courting, when it will flare up.*

**Nesting Location**

**Voice:** High-pitched *tee tee tee* followed by a lower *tew tew tew* and ending with a chatter.
**Food:** Insects, insect eggs, spiders, fruits and seeds.
**Nest/Eggs:** Deep woven cup built with moss, lichen at top and lined with small black roots and feathers, suspended from conifer branch. 5-10 eggs.

# Eastern Bluebird

*Sialia sialis*

Size Identification

Beak

Backyard Feeder

Birdhouse Nester

Nesting Location

Observation Calendar
J F M A M J J A S O N D

**Male:** Bright blue upper parts; tan throat and sides; white belly; feet and legs black.
**Female:** Similar to male except paler and head has greyish spotting.

**Voice:** Song is bright whistle *cheer cheerful charmer*. Call is lower *turrweee*.
**Food:** Variety of insects. Visits feeders for peanut butter, berries, mealworm or raisins.
**Nest/Eggs:** Built in cavity of tree or birdhouse from a variety of grasses and pine needles, lined with softer material. 3-6 eggs.

93

# Veery
*Catharus fuscescens*

**Size Identification**

**Beak**

J F M A M J J A S O N D

**Male/Female:** Overall reddish-brown upper parts; white buff chest and belly; soft tan spotting along chin and cheeks; grey sides; feet and legs pinkish-grey.

**Voice:** Soft descending notes — *turreeooreooo-reeoorreeo*. Call is a loud descending *veerr*.
**Food:** Various insects, larvae, snails, earthworms, spiders and wild berries.
**Nest/Eggs:** Built of stems, twigs and mosses lined with softer material including various grasses and rootlets. 3-5 eggs.

**Nesting Location**

**Egg: Actual Size**     94

# Wood Thrush

*Hylocichla mustelina*

Beak

**Observation Calendar**

J F M A M J J A S O N D

**Male/Female:** Rust-coloured head fades to a brown back; wings and tail dark brown with black ends; feet and legs grey with pink; white eye-ring; chin and chest white with black spotting, underparts grey.

**Voice:** Suggestive of a flute, the song is a series of varied phrases — *ee oh lee ee oh lay*.
**Food:** A variety of insects on the ground and in trees.
**Nest/Eggs:** Firm and compact cup built with grass, paper, moss, bark and mud, lined with small roots in tree or shrub, 2-15 metres above ground. 3-4 eggs.

Nesting Location

Egg: Actual Size

# American Robin

*Turdus migratorius*

Size Identification

Beak

Backyard Feeder

Observation Calendar

J F M A M J J A S O N D

**Male:** Charcoal/brown head with distinctive white above and below eyes; back and wings charcoal brown with white edges; tail dark grey; throat dark grey with thin white banding; chest and belly brick red; feet and legs black; bill yellow.
**Female:** Breast is slightly paler than male's.

**Voice:** Song is *cheerily cheerily cheerily* in a whistle tone.
**Food:** Earthworms, insects and fruit.
**Nest/Eggs:** Deep cup built with weed stalks, cloth, string and mud, lined with grass, in evergreens and deciduous trees or shrubs. 4 eggs.

Nesting Location

Egg: Actual Size

96

# Gray Catbird

*Dumetella carolinensis*

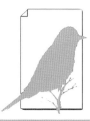

Size Identification

Beak

Observation Calendar

J F M A M J J A S O N D

**Male/Female:** Distinctive black cap with overall grey body; brick red under tail, which is hidden most of the time; feet and legs grey with hints of pink.

*Did you know? Catbirds actually migrate during the night hours and research indicates they use the moon for navigating.*

**Voice:** A distinctive cat-like *meeow* and *kwut*.
**Food:** A variety of insects, spiders and wild berries.
**Nest/Eggs:** Bulky deep cup built with twigs, vines, grass, paper and weeds lined with small roots, in dense thickets of tree or shrub, 1-3 metres above ground. 3-6 eggs.

Nesting Location

Egg: Actual Size

# Brown Thrasher

*Toxostoma rufum*

**Size Identification**

**Beak**

**Observation Calendar**

J F M A M J J A S O N D

**Male/Female:** Distinctive long black bill; grey chin, white chest and belly streaked with dark brown; long reddish-brown tail and back; reddish-brown crown on head; feet and legs pinkish-grey; white and black banding on wings.

**Voice:** Call is a loud *smack*. Voice mimics other birds and is usually repeated twice.

**Food:** Variety of insects, frogs, lizards, snakes and various wild berries.

**Nest/Eggs:** Built of twigs, sticks and dead leaves lined with softer material including grasses and rootlets. 2-6 eggs.

**Nesting Location**

# European Starling
*Sturnus vulgaris*

Size Identification

Beak

Backyard Feeder

Birdhouse Nester

Nesting Location

Observation Calendar
J F M A M J J A S O N D

**Male/Female:** *Summer:* Black iridescent bird with light white speckles over entire body; bill is sharp yellow; wing and tail are edged in white and brown; feet and legs are red. *Winter:* Speckles increase and some become brown; bill is black; feet and legs are red; wings and tail have more brown.

*Did you know? Sixty starlings were introduced into New York City in 1890. Since then they have spread throughout North America.*

**Voice:** Mimics the songs of other birds and even sounds of cats and whistles.
**Food:** A variety of insects including worms and grubs, and weed seeds.
**Nest/Eggs:** Loose cup in cavity filled with grass, leaves, cloth and feathers, up to 18 metres above the ground. 4-5 eggs.

Egg: Actual Size

# Cedar Waxwing

*Bombycilla cedrorum*

Observation Calendar

J F M A M J J A S O N D

**Male/Female:** Crested brown head with black mask running from black bill, through eyes, to behind head; white outline around mask; back brown; chest and belly yellow-brown; wings black-grey with white edges; wings and tail have red tips; rump white.

*Did you know? The name derives from the fact that their wings and tail look as though they have been dipped in red wax.*

**Voice:** Extremely high-pitched *seeee*.
**Food:** A variety of berries.
**Nest/Eggs:** Loose woven cup of grass, twigs, cotton fibre and string, lined with small roots, fine grass and down, in open wooded areas in tree or shrub, 2-6 metres above ground. 4-5 eggs.

# Blue-winged Warbler

*Vermivora pinus*

Size Identification

Beak

Observation Calendar

J F M A M J J A S O N D

**Male:** Bright yellow head, chin, chest and belly; black line through eyes; blue-black wings and tail with white banding along wings; grey back; feet and legs black; black bill.
**Female:** Similar markings to male but paler overall.

**Voice:** Low-pitched *buzzzzz* in 2 notes descending, sounds like "blue-winged."
**Food:** Variety of insects and spiders.
**Nest/Eggs:** Cup-like, built of leaves, grasses, and vines in a tangle near ground. 4-7 eggs.

Nesting Location

Egg: Actual Size

# Nashville Warbler

*Vermivora ruficapilla*

**Size Identification**

**Beak**

**Observation Calendar**

J F M A M J J A S O N D

**Male/Female:** Thin, very pointed bill; head and neck bluish grey; eye-ring white; upper parts olive green; underparts yellow, white on belly.

**Voice:** Calls include *see it see it see it*, and *ti ti ti ti ti*.
**Food:** A variety of insects.
**Nest/Eggs:** Nest of moss or bark lined with grass and hair, on ground. 4-5 eggs.

**Nesting Location**

# Yellow Warbler

*Dendroica petechia*

Size Identification

Beak

## Observation Calendar

J F M A M J J A S O N D

**Male:** Yellow throat and chest; olive back; wings and tail dark olive with yellow highlights; chest barred with chestnut stripes; bill and feet reddish black.
**Female:** Similar to male only darker and lacks chestnut markings below.

**Voice:** A sweet and rapid *tsee, tsee, tsee, tsee, titi-wee.*
**Food:** Insects with large quantities of caterpillars, beetles and moths. Young birds are fed earthworms as well.
**Nest/Eggs:** Cup of milkweed, hair, down and fine grasses, built in upright fork of tree or bush. 3-6 eggs.

Nesting Location

Egg: Actual Size

# Chestnut-sided Warbler

*Dendroica pensylvanica*

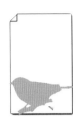

Observation Calendar
J F M A M J J A S O N D

**Male:** Bright lemon-yellow crown with chestnut down sides of breast; black band running through eyes from black bill; black and white banding on back with yellow tinting; wings and tail black with white edges; feet and legs black; chin and belly white.

**Female:** Similar to male except mask is duller and chestnut on sides is reduced.

*Did you know? Audubon found these birds to be rare, but with the clearing of woodland, sightings have increased.*

**Voice:** A territorial song — *sweet sweet sweet I so sweet.*

**Food:** A variety of insects including caterpillars, moths and beetles.

**Nest/Eggs:** Loose cup of stems, grass and plant down, lined with grass and hair, in briar tangles, hedges or shrubs, up to 2 metres above ground. 3-5 eggs.

# Magnolia Warbler

*Dendroica magnolia*

Observation Calendar
J F M A M J J A S O N D

**Male:** Grey head with small eyebrow stripe of white above eyes; black mask; yellow chin; chest and belly yellow with black banding; back grey with black; wings and tail grey with white edges; two white wing bars; white rump.

**Female**: Similar to male except banding on chest is narrower; face is grey without black mask and white eyebrow; white eye-ring.

**Voice:** A short melodic song — *weeta weeta weeta wee.*
**Food:** A variety of insects and spiders.
**Nest/Eggs:** Nest is a loosely built cup of grass, moss and weed stalks, lined with dark roots, in small conifers along the edge of wooded areas and in gardens. 3-5 eggs.

# Black-throated Blue Warbler

*Dendroica caerulescens*

## Observation Calendar

J F M A M J J A S O N D

**Male:** Blue-grey head and back; black face mask with black bill; chest white; wings and tail black with white edges; feet and legs black.

**Female:** Olive-brown head, back and wings with lighter tone on chin, chest and belly; black bill; thin buff eyebrows; feet and legs black; wings and tail olive-brown with white edges.

**Voice:** A husky song, "I am soo lazzzzy," and a call that is a flat *tip*.

**Food:** A variety of insects, fruits and seeds taken mainly on ground or low lying branches.

**Nest/Eggs:** Bulky cup of spiderweb, dead wood, twigs, leaves and grass, lined with dark rootlets in tree or shrub close to ground. 3-5 eggs.

# Yellow-rumped Warbler

*Dendroica coronata*

**Observation Calendar**
J F M A M J J A S O N D

**Male/Female:** *Spring:* Yellow rump and yellow patch on either side of chest; yellow crown set against grey head; black mask running from black bill; back grey with black banding; wings and tail black with white edges; two white wing bars; chin white; chest white with black band; feet and legs charcoal; white eyebrows. *Fall:* Similar but duller markers, no black mask, more brown and buff overall.

**Voice:** Song is light musical notes. Call is *cheeeck.*
**Food:** A variety of insects and fruit.
**Nest/Eggs:** Deep cup of twigs, bark, plant down and fibres, lined with hair feather and fine grass, in tree or shrub near trunk. 3-5 eggs.

# Black-throated Green Warbler

*Dendroica virens*

**Observation Calendar**
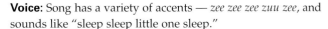
J F M A M J J A S O N D

**Male:** Olive head and back; yellow around eyes and on cheeks; black throat and chest changing to speckled black on white on belly and chest; black banding along sides of belly; wings and tail are black with white edging; two white bars on wings; feet and legs brown-black; white vent at base of tail.
**Female:** Yellow on throat with minimal black.

**Voice:** Song has a variety of accents — *zee zee zee zuu zee*, and sounds like "sleep sleep little one sleep."
**Food:** Variety of insects and fruit.
**Nest/Eggs:** Compact cup of fine bark, twigs, grass, lichens and spiderweb, lined with hair, fur, feathers and small roots, in tree or shrub, 1-25 metres above ground. 3-5 eggs.

# Pine Warbler
*Dendroica pinus*

Beak

Backyard Feeder

J F M A M J J A S O N D

**Male:** Bright yellow chin, chest and belly; dark wings with white banding; short black pointed beak; light streaking along sides; green head and back; tail black with yellow highlights; feet and legs dark; yellow ring around eyes.
**Female:** Dull greyish brown head and back; yellowish chin, chest and belly.

**Voice:** Melodic trill. Call is *chiiip*.
**Food:** Insects, spiders, fruit, berries and pine seeds.
**Nest/Eggs:** Pine needles shaped into cup along with pieces of bark and weeds. Always in a pine tree. 3-5 eggs.

Nesting Location

Egg: Actual Size

# Black-and-white Warbler

*Mniotilta varia*

**Size Identification**

**Beak**

Observation Calendar
J F M A M J J A S O N D

**Male:** Black-and-white striped from crown down entire body length; feet and legs charcoal; bill is thin and black with thin yellow line at mouth opening.
**Female:** Similar to the male except striping on chest and belly is grey and white, throat is white.

*Did you know? The Black-and-white Warbler is one of the earliest migrants to return in spring.*

**Voice:** Seven or more squeaky calls — *weesee, weesee, weesee, weesee, weesee, weesee, weesee.*
**Food:** A variety of insects, mainly gypsy moths and tent caterpillars.
**Nest/Eggs:** Cup built of leaves, grass, hair and bark, at base of tree or near a boulder. 4-5 eggs.

**Nesting Location**

**Egg: Actual Size** 110

# American Redstart
*Setophaga ruticilla*

Size Identification

Beak

Observation Calendar

J F M A M J J A S O N D

**Male:** Black overall with large orange bands on wings and outer tail feathers; bright red/orange patch on side of chest; belly white; feet and legs black.
**Female:** Overall olive-grey with large yellow bands on wings and tail; white eye-ring, broken; yellow on sides of white chest; white belly; feet and legs black.

**Voice:** Song is a series of high-pitched thin notes ending downward. Call is *chip*.
**Food:** A variety of insects, wild berries and seeds.
**Nest/Eggs:** Compact woven cup built with plant down and grass, lined with weeds, hair and feathers, covered on the outside with lichens, plant down and spiderweb, in woodlands and swamps. 4 eggs.

Nesting Location

Egg: Actual Size

# Ovenbird
*Seiurus aurocapillus*

**Beak**

Observation Calendar
J F M A M J J A S O N D

**Male/Female:** Olive overall with distinctive mark on head that is orange outlined in black, running from bill to the back of the neck; chest white with black speckles; bill dark on top with yellow on underside; black eyes surrounded by white.

**Voice:** A progressively louder *teecher, teecher, teecher, teecher.*
**Food:** Snails, slugs, worms, spiders and most other insects.
**Nest/Eggs:** Covered bowl, with side entry made of dead leaves, grass, moss and bark, lined with small roots, fibres and hair, on ground in depression. 3-5 eggs.

**Nesting Location**

# Common Yellowthroat

*Geothlypis trichas*

Observation Calendar

J F M A M J J A S O N D

**Male:** Yellow chin, chest and belly contrast with a dark black mask, which runs from bill, around eyes, to lower neck; white line blends into an olive head, back, wings and tail; feet and legs grey.

**Female:** Light brown without the distinctive mask.

**Voice:** A very high-pitched song — *witchity, witchity, witchity* — that is heavily accented.

**Food:** Caterpillars, beetles, ants and other small insects.

**Nest/Eggs:** Bulky cup of grass, reeds, leaves and moss, lined with grass and hair, on or near ground, in weed stalks or low bushes. 3-5 eggs.

113

# Scarlet Tanager
*Piranga olivacea*

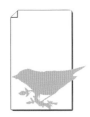

Observation Calendar
J F M A M J J A S O N D

**Male:** Scarlet red from head to rump with dark black wings and tail; bill is pale grey; feet and legs dark.
**Female:** Olive-yellow overall with black-grey wings and tail.

**Voice:** Call is a *chip burr*, while its song is a buzzing *querit, queer, queery, querit, queer* that is well spaced out.
**Food:** A variety of insects and fruit.
**Nest/Eggs:** Stout cup nest on farthest branches in tree or shrub, sometimes far from the ground. 3-5 eggs.

# Eastern Towhee

*Pipilo erythrophthalmus*

**Observation Calendar**

J F M A M J J A S O N D

**Male:** Distinctive black head with black bill; rust-red sides and vent; white belly; feet and legs pinkish-grey; black back with white banding; long black tail with white oval-shaped underparts.
**Female:** Similar to male but with brown head, back and tail; white belly.

**Voice:** Whistle followed by a trill in 2 notes. Sounds like *"drink your tea."* Call is a quick *chewink*.
**Food:** Variety of insects, snakes, lizards, weeds and spiders.
**Nest/Eggs:** Built of twigs and leaves with softer grasses lining inside placed in depression in ground. 2-6 eggs.

# American Tree Sparrow

*Spizella arborea*

Observation Calendar

J F M A M J J A S O N D

**Male/Female:** Rust on top of head with light grey face, rust band running through eyes; chin, chest and belly grey with a faint dark grey spot on chest; wings and tail brown and black with white edge; two white wing bars; short pointed bill is grey on top with yellow underside; feet and legs are red-black; rump grey.

**Voice:** Call is *te el wit*.
**Food:** A variety of weed seeds and tree seeds.
**Nest/Eggs:** Cup nest, low in tree and shrub. 4 eggs.

116

# Chipping Sparrow

*Spizella passerina*

Beak

Backyard Feeder

Observation Calendar

J F M A M J J A S O N D

**Male/Female:** *Summer:* Bright rust crown with grey face that has a black band running through each eye; short pointed bill is black; chin white changing to grey for chest and belly; feet and legs pink; white eyebrows; wings and tail dark with brown and white edges; brown banding with black on back. *Winter:* Rust crown becomes duller, turning brown with black streaks; bill is pale yellow and black; eyebrows change to buff; underside changes to buff.

**Voice:** Song is short trill.

**Food:** A variety of insects on the ground and occasionally snatches flying insects.

**Nest/Eggs:** Cup built with grass, weed stalks and small roots, lined with hair and grass, low in tree or shrub, up to 8 metres above ground. 4 eggs.

Nesting Location

Egg: Actual Size

# Field Sparrow
*Spizella pusilla*

**Size Identification**

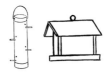

**Beak**

**Backyard Feeder**

Observation Calendar
J F M A M J J A S O N D

**Male/Female:** Overall brown with grey speckles; reddish-brown cap; distinctive white eye-ring; bright pink bill; feet and legs pinkish-grey; tail dark with brown highlights; white vent and lower belly.

**Voice:** Whistles descending and gradually increasing in speed. Calls are *chip* and trills.
**Food:** Various insects and seeds. May visit feeders if seeds have fallen to ground.
**Nest/Eggs:** Cup-like, built from a variety of grasses and positioned on ground. 3-4 eggs.

**Nesting Location**

# Vesper Sparrow

*Pooecetes gramineus*

**Size Identification**

**Beak**

**Backyard Feeder**

### Observation Calendar
J F M A M J J A S O N D

**Male/Female:** Light grey overall with very fine streaks of black running down entire body; short pointed bill; feet and legs grey; back banded with black; wings and tail dark grey with white edges; white eye-ring, and small chestnut patch near shoulder; white tail feathers are revealed in flight.

*Did you know? The Vesper Sparrow earned its name from its song that may be heard in the evening — at vespers, when evening prayers were said in the monasteries.*

**Voice:** A whistle of two beats, with the second being higher, followed by trills.
**Food:** A variety of insects, weed seeds and grains.
**Nest/Eggs:** Depression in ground filled with grass, stalks and small roots, and lined with the same. 4 eggs.

**Nesting Location**

119

**Egg: Actual Size**

# Savannah Sparrow

*Passerculus sandwichensis*

**Observation Calendar**
J F M A M J J A S O N D

**Male/Female:** Black, brown and white stripe on head; back brown with black banding; chin and chest streaked with black and brown; wings and tail black with brown edges; tail is notched; bright yellow eyebrows; feet and legs red; short pointed bill; white eye-ring.

**Voice:** A faint, lisping *tsit tsit tsit tseeeee tsaaaay.*
**Food:** Main diet consists of weed seeds, but will eat a variety of insects, spiders and snails.
**Nest/Eggs:** Scratched hollow in ground filled with grass, lined with finer grass, hair and small roots. 3-6 eggs.

# Song Sparrow

*Melospiza melodia*

Size Identification

Beak

Backyard Feeder

Observation Calendar

J F M A M J J A S O N D

**Male/Female:** Brown head and back streaked with black; whitish eyebrows extending to back of neck; brown band running through eyes; chin, chest and belly are white with brown-black banding running down to lower belly; short pointed bill is brown on top with paler underside; red-brown crown with central white stripe; wings and tail brown with white edges; feet and legs pale brown; long rounded tail.

*Did you know? Thoreau interpreted this sparrow's song as "Maids! Maids! Maids! hang up your teakettle-ettle-ettle."*

**Voice:** A variety of calls including *tsip* and *tchump*. Song is a variety of rich notes.
**Food:** Various insects, weed seeds and fruit.
**Nest/Eggs:** Cup close to ground made with weeds, leaves and bark, lined with grass roots and hair, in tree or shrub, less than 4 metres from ground. 3-5 eggs.

Nesting Location

Egg: Actual Size

# Swamp Sparrow
*Melospiza georgiana*

### Observation Calendar
J F M A M J J A S O N D

**Male/Female**: *Summer:* Top of head is reddish brown and black; black line through each eye; pale grey eyebrows; black bill is small and sharp; chin and chest white-grey with rust along sides; back brown with black banding; wings and tail feathers brown with black ends and white edges; feet and legs pink. *Winter:* Similar to summer but both sides of chest turn darker brown and top of head is streaked with black and brown with grey central stripe.

Put on your hip waders to spot this bird. They spend their summers near swamps and bogs.

**Voice:** Song is an unbroken musical trill. Call is *chip*.
**Food:** A variety of insects and seeds.
**Nest/Eggs:** Bulky cup built with grass, lined with finer grass, in tussock of grass or in low shrub. 3-6 eggs.

# White-throated Sparrow

*Zonotrichia albicollis*

Beak

Backyard Feeder

Observation Calendar

J F M A M J J A S O N D

**Male/Female:** Top of head is black with white central stripe; white eyebrows on either side with yellow tint at base of bill; black band running through eyes followed by grey cheeks; small white bib under chin; grey chest; grey belly with faint banding; wings and tail feathers black and brown with white edges; back brown-banded with black.

**Voice:** Whistle is *teeet teeet tetodi tetodi teetodi*. Calls are *tseet*.
**Food:** A variety of insects, grains, weed seeds and fruit.
**Nest/Eggs:** Cup built of grass, small roots, pine needles, twigs, bark and moss, lined with small roots, hair and grass. 3-5 eggs.

Nesting Location

123

Egg: Actual Size

# Dark-eyed Junco

*Junco hyemalis*

**Size Identification**

**Beak**

**Backyard Feeder**

Observation Calendar
J F M A M J J A S O N D

**Male:** Dark charcoal overall with white belly; short sharp bill; feet and legs pink; tail has white outer feathers that can be seen in flight.
**Female:** May be slightly paler than male.

**Nesting Location**

*Did you know? Although there are many different sub-species, the slate-coloured is the only one found in the region.*

**Voice:** Song is a trill in short phrases. Calls are *tsip, zeeet* or *keew keew.*
**Food:** A variety of insects, weed seeds and wild fruit.
**Nest/Eggs:** Large and compact nest built with grass, rootlets and hair, lined with hair, concealed low to or on the ground. 4-5 eggs.

# Northern Cardinal

*Cardinalis cardinalis*

Observation Calendar
J F M A M J J A S O N D

**Male:** Brilliant red overall with a stout red-orange bill, crested head; black mask beginning at base of bill resembling a small bib; feet dark red.

**Female:** Buff and grey with hints of bright red on crest, wings and back. Stout red-orange bill with black mask beginning at base of bill (bib may appear smaller), feet are dark red.

*Did you know? The cardinal gets its name from its bright red colour, which resembles that of the robes and hat of a Roman Catholic cardinal.*

**Voice:** Song is a series of repeated whistles — *wheit wheit wheit, cheer cheer cheer.* Also *chip.*

**Food:** Seeds, fruits, grains and various insects.

**Nest/Eggs:** Woven cup of twigs, vines, leaves and grass, 2-3 metres above ground, in dense shrubbery. 2-5 eggs.

# Rose-breasted Grosbeak
*Pheucticus ludovicianus*

**Size Identification**

**Beak**

**Backyard Feeder**

Observation Calendar
J F M A M J J A S O N D

**Male:** Large, pale bill with black head; red V shape on chest; belly white with rust on either side close to wing; wings and tail black; white at edges of tail feathers visible in flight; white patches on wings; rump white; feet and legs charcoal.
**Female:** Buff eyebrows that extend to back of neck; brown head and back with shade of black; wings and tail brown with white edges; two white wing bars; chest and belly streaked brown; feet and legs charcoal.

**Nesting Location**

*Did you know? The Rose-breasted Grosbeak is a fierce competitor when mating, clashing violently with other males. However, when it comes time to sitting on the nest, the males have been known to sing.*

**Voice:** Similar to a robin, but rapid notes that are a continuous *cheer-e-ly cheer-e-ly.* Call is *chink chink.*
**Food:** A variety of insects, tree buds, fruit and wild seeds.
**Nest/Eggs:** Woven grass cup in fork of deciduous tree or shrub, close to the ground. 3-6 eggs.

# Indigo Bunting
*Passerina cyanea*

Beak

Observation Calendar

J F M A M J J A S O N D

**Male:** Medium to deep turquoise blue overall; wide, sharp, grey beak; feet and legs black; wings and tail dark with blue highlights.
**Female:** Soft brown overall; buff sides and belly; faint wing bands; short conical grey beak.

**Voice:** Rapid series of whistles that are short and paired together — *tse tsee tew tew*. Call is short *spiit*.
**Food:** Insects, seeds, grain, berries.
**Nest/Eggs:** Compact woven cup built from stems, grasses and leaves, lined with down in thick vegetation. 2-6 eggs.

Nesting Location

Egg: Actual Size

# Bobolink
*Dolichonyx oryzivorus*

**Size Identification**

**Beak**

Observation Calendar

J F M A M J J A S O N D

**Male:** *Summer:* Black overall with pale yellow patch on back of head; back black changing to large white patch down to rump; wings have white patches and edges; bill black. In flight: white rump is revealed. Tail has sharp pointed feathers.
**Female/Male:** *Winter:* brown and buff overall with black streaks over top of head; legs red.

*Did you know? These birds need a hayfield habitat to survive. Studies show that most of the young will die when farmers' fields are mown before they have a chance to fledge.*

**Nesting Location**

**Voice:** Song is a light phrase that increases in pitch and has been described as *Bob o link, bob o link spink spank spink.* Usually sings in flight. Call is metallic *clink.*
**Food:** A variety of insects and weed seeds.
**Nest/Eggs:** Slight hollow in ground with bulky gathering of grass and weed stalks. Lined with fine grass in areas near water and within waterside plants. 4-7 eggs.

# Red-winged Blackbird

*Agelaius phoeniceus*

Beak

Backyard Feeder

Observation Calendar

J F M A M J J A S O N D

**Male:** Black overall with distinctive red shoulder patch bordered with light yellow at bottom.
**Female:** Brown with buff eyebrows and chin; chest and belly buff streaked with dark brown; wings and tail feathers brown with buff edges.

*Did you know? Red-winged Blackbirds are prolific breeders, sometimes breeding three times in one season. They are seen in freshwater marshes.*

**Voice:** Song is *ocaaleee ocaalee*.
**Food:** A variety of insects and weed seeds.
**Nest/Eggs:** Bulky cup built of leaves, rushes, grass, rootlets, moss and milkweed fibre, lined with grass, in tall waterside plants. 3-4 eggs.

Nesting Location

129

Egg: Actual Size

# Eastern Meadowlark
*Sturnella magna*

**Beak**

**Backyard Feeder**

**Birdhouse Nester**

**Nesting Location**

Observation Calendar

J F M A M J J A S O N D

**Male/Female:** Bright yellow chin and throat separated by a V-shaped black collar; black on top of head with grey cheeks; yellow and black band runs through eyes; sides white with black sidebars; back and wings black and brown with white edges; feet and legs grey; pale bill is long and thin with grey underside.

**Voice:** Song is *teee yuuu teee yaar* repeated 2-8 times.
**Food:** A variety of insects including grubs, beetles, grasshoppers and caterpillars. Also eats seeds and grains.
**Nest/Eggs:** Bulky cup in hollow on the ground in pastures, fields and marshes. Dome-shaped with a roof of interwoven grasses. 3-5 eggs.

# Common Grackle

*Quiscalus quiscula*

Beak

Backyard Feeder

Observation Calendar
J F M A M J J A S O N D

**Male:** Overall iridescent black and purple; bright yellow eyes; black bill long and sharp; feet and legs are charcoal grey; long tail.
**Female:** Similar but duller iridescent colouring, tail is shorter.

*Did you know? Flocks in the thousands gather on fields and cause a lot of damage to farmers' crops.*

**Voice:** Chatter is a metallic and rasping *grideleeeeek*. Calls are *chak chah*.
**Food:** A variety of ground insects, seeds, grains, minnows, rodents and crayfish.
**Nest/Eggs:** Loose bulky cup built with weed stalks, twigs, grass, debris, lined with feather and grass, in conifer trees or shrubs. Will occasionally use an osprey's nest. Prefers to nest in colonies. 3-6 eggs.

Nesting Location

Egg: Actual Size

# Brown-headed Cowbird

*Molothrus ater*

Observation Calendar

J F M A M J J A S O N D

**Male:** Brown head, glossy black overall; feet and legs black; sharp black bill.
**Female:** Overall grey with dark brown wings and tail; faint buff streaking on chest down to lower belly, feet and legs are black.

*Did you know? Molothrus ater, the Cowbird's scientific name, means dark, greedy beggar, an apt name for a bird that leaves its eggs for other birds to hatch.*

**Voice:** A squeaky *weee titi.*
**Food:** A variety of insects, weed seeds, grains and grass.
**Nest/Eggs:** Lays eggs in nests of other birds. 1 egg.

# Orchard Oriole
*Icterus spurius*

Size Identification

Beak

Backyard Feeder

Observation Calendar
J F M A M J J A S O N D

**Male:** Black head and back; long, sharp black beak; chestnut belly and rump; long black tail; feet and legs black; black wings with one wing bar.
**Female:** Olive-green overall; yellow belly and chest; wings black with two wing bars.

**Voice:** Quick progression of whistled notes. Call is a quick *chuck*.
**Food:** Insects, fruit, sugar solutions and tree blossoms.
**Nest/Eggs:** Suspended pouch woven with grass and lined with fine material. 3-7 eggs.

Nesting Location

Egg: Actual Size

# Baltimore Oriole
*Icterus galbula*

**Size Identification**

**Beak**

**Backyard Feeder**

Observation Calendar
J F M A M J J A S O N D

**Male:** Black head; bright orange body; black wings with orange spur and white banding; tail is black with orange along edges; legs and feet grey; long sharp grey beak.
**Female:** Browner than male with olive-yellow on rump; orange-yellow chest and belly; head and back mix of black, orange and brown; throat blotched; tail brown-orange.

*Did you know? Baltimore Orioles can be attracted to feeders with orange slices or sugar solutions.*

**Nesting Location**

**Voice:** Song is a note whistled 4-8 times. Call is a two-note *teetoo* and rapid chatter *ch ch ch ch*.
**Food:** Insects, flower nectar, fruit.
**Nest/Eggs:** Plant fibre that hangs from branches. 4-6 eggs.

# House Finch

*Carpodacus mexicanus*

Size Identification

Beak

Backyard Feeder

Observation Calendar

J F M A M J J A S O N D

**Male:** Red crown, chin and chest, which changes to buff at belly; wings and tail brown; feet and legs grey; grey bill; white undertail; dark brown banding around the sides.
**Female:** All greyish brown with faint banding down the sides.

**Voice:** Musical warble ending with *jeeeeer.*
**Food:** Weed seeds, fruit, buds.
**Nest/Eggs:** Cup of lined weed and grass, roots, feathers, string and twigs, 1-2 metres above ground. 4-5 eggs.

Nesting Location

Egg: Actual Size

# American Goldfinch

*Carduelis tristis*

**Size Identification**

**Beak**

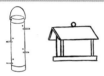

**Backyard Feeder**

Observation Calendar
J F M A M J J A S O N D

**Male:** *Summer:* Bright yellow overall with black forehead and yellow bill; black wings with white bands; tail black with white edges; rump white; feet and legs red. *Winter:* Similar, but bright yellow is replaced by grey with hints of yellow.
**Female/Male:** *Winter:* Similar except overall olive brown with yellow highlights.

**Voice:** Sing as they fly with a succession of chips and twitters, *per chic o ree per chic o ree.*
**Food:** A variety of insects, but mostly interested in thistle and weed seeds.
**Nest/Eggs:** Neat cup built with fibres woven together, lined with thistle and feather down, in leafy tree or shrubs in upright branches, 1-5 metres above ground. 4-6 eggs.

**Nesting Location**

**Egg: Actual Size**     136

# House Sparrow
*Passer domesticus*

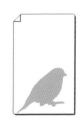

**Size Identification**

**Beak**

**Backyard Feeder**

**Birdhouse Nester**

**Nesting Location**

Observation Calendar

J F M A M J J A S O N D

**Male:** Grey crown with rich brown from eye to back; white cheeks; wings and tail striped with black; two distinct white wing bands; rump grey; throat and chest black, which turns grey at belly; bill black; feet and legs pink.
**Female:** Dull brown with buff chin, chest and belly; light buff-coloured eyebrows and yellow/grey bill.

*Did you know? In 1850, 8 pairs of House Sparrows were brought to North America from Europe to help control cankerworms in crops. The first attempt failed, but this sparrow has now become one of the most common birds in cities and towns.*

**Voice:** Repeated *chureep, chirup.*
**Food:** Insects, seeds, grains and food waste.
**Nest/Eggs:** Takes over nests from other birds. Usually a large untidy ball of grass, weeds, some hair, feathers. 3-7 eggs.

**Egg: Actual Size**

# Checklist of Birds

This checklist follows the same sequence as the book. Use these pages to record the date and place of bird sightings.

☐ Common Loon *18*
Date: _____
Place: _____

☐ Double-crested
Cormorant *19*
Date: _____
Place: _____

☐ Great Blue Heron *20*
Date: _____
Place: _____

☐ Turkey Vulture *21*
Date: _____
Place: _____

☐ Canada Goose *22*
Date: _____
Place: _____

☐ Mute Swan *23*
Date: _____
Place: _____

☐ Tundra Swan *24*
Date: _____
Place: _____

☐ Wood Duck *25*
Date: _____
Place: _____

☐ Gadwall *26*
Date: _____
Place: _____

☐ American Wigeon *27*
Date: _____
Place: _____

☐ American Black Duck *28*
Date: _____
Place: _____

☐ Mallard *29*
Date: _____
Place: _____

☐ Blue-winged Teal *30*
Date: _____
Place: _____

☐ Northern Pintail *31*
Date: _____
Place: _____

☐ Green-winged Teal *32*
Date: _____
Place: _____

☐ Ring-necked Duck *33*
Date: _____
Place: _____

☐ Bufflehead *34*
Date: _____
Place: _____

☐ Hooded Merganser *35*
Date: _____
Place: _____

☐ Common Merganser *36*
Date: _____
Place: _____

☐ Ruddy Duck *37*
Date: _____
Place: _____

☐ Osprey *38*
Date: _____
Place: _____

☐ Bald Eagle *39*
Date: _____
Place: _____

☐ Sharp-shinned Hawk *40*
Date: _____
Place: _____

☐ Red-tailed Hawk *41*
Date: _____
Place: _____

☐ Rough-legged Hawk *42*
Date: _____
Place: _____

☐ American Kestrel *43*
Date: _____
Place: _____

☐ Peregrine Falcon *44*
Date: _____
Place: _____

☐ Ring-necked Pheasant *45*
Date: _____
Place: _____

☐ Ruffed Grouse *46*
Date: _____
Place: _____

☐ Wild Turkey *47*
Date: _____
Place: _____

☐ Virginia Rail *48*
Date: _____
Place: _____

☐ Sora *49*
Date: _____
Place: _____

☐ American Coot *50*
Date: _____
Place: _____

☐ Killdeer *51*
Date: _____
Place: _____

☐ Spotted Sandpiper *52*
Date: _____
Place: _____

☐ Ring-billed Gull *53*
Date: _____
Place: _____

☐ Herring Gull *54*
Date: _____
Place: _____

☐ Great Black-backed Gull *55*
Date: _____
Place: _____

☐ Rock Dove *56*
Date: _____
Place: _____

☐ Mourning Dove *57*
Date: _____
Place: _____

☐ Black-billed Cuckoo *58*
Date: _____
Place: _____

☐ Yellow-billed Cuckoo *59*
Date: _____
Place: _____

☐ Eastern Screech-Owl *60*
Date: _____
Place: _____

☐ Great Horned Owl *61*
Date: _____
Place: _____

☐ Chimney Swift *62*
Date: _____
Place: _____

☐ Ruby-throated Hummingbird *63*
Date: _____
Place: _____

☐ Belted Kingfisher *64*
Date: _____
Place: _____

☐ Red-headed Woodpecker 65
Date: _____
Place: _____

☐ Red-bellied Woodpecker 66
Date: _____
Place: _____

☐ Downy Woodpecker 67
Date: _____
Place: _____

☐ Hairy Woodpecker 68
Date: _____
Place: _____

☐ Northern Flicker 69
Date: _____
Place: _____

☐ Eastern Wood-Pewee 70
Date: _____
Place: _____

☐ Least Flycatcher 71
Date: _____
Place: _____

☐ Eastern Phoebe 72
Date: _____
Place: _____

☐ Great Crested Flycatcher 73
Date: _____
Place: _____

☐ Eastern Kingbird 74
Date: _____
Place: _____

☐ Warbling Vireo 75
Date: _____
Place: _____

☐ Red-eyed Vireo 76
Date: _____
Place: _____

☐ Blue Jay 77
Date: _____
Place: _____

☐ American Crow 78
Date: _____
Place: _____

☐ Horned Lark 79
Date: _____
Place: _____

☐ Purple Martin 80
Date: _____
Place: _____

☐ Tree Swallow 81
Date: _____
Place: _____

☐ Northern Rough-winged Swallow 82
Date: _____
Place: _____

☐ Bank Swallow 83
Date: _____
Place: _____

☐ Cliff Swallow 84
Date: _____
Place: _____

☐ Barn Swallow 85
Date: _____
Place: _____

☐ Black-capped Chickadee 86
Date: _____
Place: _____

☐ Red-breasted Nuthatch 87
Date: _____
Place: _____

☐ White-breasted Nuthatch 88
Date: _____
Place: _____

☐ Brown Creeper *89*
Date: _____
Place: _____

☐ House Wren *90*
Date: _____
Place: _____

☐ Golden-crowned Kinglet *91*
Date: _____
Place: _____

☐ Ruby-crowned Kinglet *92*
Date: _____
Place: _____

☐ Eastern Bluebird *93*
Date: _____
Place: _____

☐ Veery *94*
Date: _____
Place: _____

☐ Wood Thrush *95*
Date: _____
Place: _____

☐ American Robin *96*
Date: _____
Place: _____

☐ Gray Catbird *97*
Date: _____
Place: _____

☐ Brown Thrasher *98*
Date: _____
Place: _____

☐ European Starling *99*
Date: _____
Place: _____

☐ Cedar Waxwing *100*
Date: _____
Place: _____

☐ Blue-winged Warbler *101*
Date: _____
Place: _____

☐ Nashville Warbler *102*
Date: _____
Place: _____

☐ Yellow Warbler *103*
Date: _____
Place: _____

☐ Chestnut-sided Warbler *104*
Date: _____
Place: _____

☐ Magnolia Warbler *105*
Date: _____
Place: _____

☐ Black-throated Blue Warbler *106*
Date: _____
Place: _____

☐ Yellow-rumped Warbler *107*
Date: _____
Place: _____

☐ Black-throated Green Warbler *108*
Date: _____
Place: _____

☐ Pine Warbler *109*
Date: _____
Place: _____

☐ Black-and-white Warbler *110*
Date: _____
Place: _____

☐ American Redstart *111*
Date: _____
Place: _____

☐ Ovenbird *112*
Date: _____
Place: _____

☐ Common Yellowthroat *113*
Date: _____
Place: _____

**Checklist of Birds**

☐ Scarlet Tanager *114*
Date: _____
Place: _____

☐ Eastern Towhee *115*
Date: _____
Place: _____

☐ American Tree
Sparrow *116*
Date: _____
Place: _____

☐ Chipping Sparrow *117*
Date: _____
Place: _____

☐ Field Sparrow *118*
Date: _____
Place: _____

☐ Vesper Sparrow *119*
Date: _____
Place: _____

☐ Savannah Sparrow *120*
Date: _____
Place: _____

☐ Song Sparrow *121*
Date: _____
Place: _____

☐ Swamp Sparrow *122*
Date: _____
Place: _____

☐ White-throated
Sparrow *123*
Date: _____
Place: _____

☐ Dark-eyed Junco *124*
Date: _____
Place: _____

☐ Northern Cardinal *125*
Date: _____
Place: _____

☐ Rose-breasted
Grosbeak *126*
Date: _____
Place: _____

☐ Indigo Bunting *127*
Date: _____
Place: _____

☐ Bobolink *128*
Date: _____
Place: _____

☐ Red-winged Blackbird *129*
Date: _____
Place: _____

☐ Eastern Meadowlark *130*
Date: _____
Place: _____

☐ Common Grackle *131*
Date: _____
Place: _____

☐ Brown-headed Cowbird
*132*
Date: _____
Place: _____

☐ Orchard Oriole *133*
Date: _____
Place: _____

☐ Baltimore Oriole *134*
Date: _____
Place: _____

☐ House Finch *135*
Date: _____
Place: _____

☐ American Goldfinch *136*
Date: _____
Place: _____

☐ House Sparrow *137*
Date: _____
Place: _____

# Index